TECHNOLOGY
TIPS FOR SENIORS
VOLUME 2.0

JEFFREY ALLEN – ASHLEY HALLENE

AMERICAN BAR ASSOCIATION
Senior Lawyers
Division

Cover design by Cory Ottenwess/ABA Design

The materials contained herein represent the opinions of the authors and/or the editors, and should not be construed to be the views or opinions of the law firms or companies with whom such persons are in partnership with, associated with, or employed by, nor of the American Bar Association or the Senior Lawyers Division unless adopted pursuant to the bylaws of the Association.

Nothing contained in this book is to be considered as the rendering of legal advice for specific cases, and readers are responsible for obtaining such advice from their own legal counsel. This book is intended for educational and informational purposes only.

p. 50 Mr. Coffee® Mug Warmer photo courtesy Newell Brands Inc.
p. 67 Bamboo Charging Stand photo courtesy MobileVision® by CE Supply
p. 128 Orbi™ WiFi system photo courtesy NETGEAR®

Printed in the United States of America.

22 21 20 19 18 5 4 3 2 1

Library of Congress Cataloging-in-Publication Data

Names: Allen, Jeffrey (Jeffrey Michael), author. | Hallene, Ashley, author. |
      American Bar Association. Senior Lawyers Division, sponsoring body.
Title: Tech tips for seniors / by Jeffrey Allen and Ashley Hallene.
Other titles: Technology tips for seniors
Description: Second edition. | Chicago : American Bar Association, 2018.
Identifiers: LCCN 2018032908 | ISBN 9781641052627 (print : alk. paper)
Subjects: LCSH: Computers and older people. | Internet and older people. |
      Technology and older people.
Classification: LCC QA76.9.O43 A45 2018 | DDC 004.084/6—dc23
LC record available at https://lccn.loc.gov/2018032908

Discounts are available for books ordered in bulk. Special consideration is given to state bars, CLE programs, and other bar-related organizations. Inquire at Book Publishing, ABA Publishing, American Bar Association, 321 N. Clark Street, Chicago, Illinois 60654-7598.

www.ShopABA.org

Table of Contents

INTRODUCTION

A BRIEF HISTORY OF THE RECENT EVOLUTION OF TECHNOLOGY

In the beginning of law office technology, there was the personal computer . . . and it was good. Technically, e-mail was on the scene before the personal computer. But without a personal computer and means to access it, who would know?

The display panel for Herman Hollerith's (whose company became IBM) tabulating machine for the 1890 census.
Image courtesy of Michael Hicks on Flickr

Before all this we had the tabulating machine of 1891, an electromechanical machine built to assist in summarizing the information stored on punch cards. The machine was invented by Herman Hollerith, a former Census Office employee who developed it to help process the data from the 1890 U.S. census. Hollerith went on to found the Tabulating Machine Company. In 1911, this company would merge with three other companies (International Time Recording Company, Computing Scale Company of America, and Bundy Manufacturing Company), forming the Computing-Tabulating-Recording Company (CTR). All four companies' combined revenue for fiscal year 1910 was greater than $950,000.

By 1924, CTR became International Business Machines (aka IBM). All the while, the company was refining and improving its business machines. At this point they had the Carroll Rotary Press, a system that produced punch cards at previously unheard of speeds. By 1931, the company offered the first Hollerith punch card machine that could multiply (the Hollerith 600 Multiplying Punch) and the first Hollerith alphabetical accounting machine. That same year saw the first "super computing machine," a term coined by the *New York World* to describe the Columbia Difference Tabulator, a tabulator-based machine made for the

Columbia Statistical Bureau. The machine itself was so massive it was nicknamed "Packard." Fast forward to 1964, and IBM introduces the IBM Magnetic Tape Selectric Typewriter, a product that began the application of magnetic recording devices to typewriting, and eventually gave rise to desktop word processing. 1971 saw the first application of speech recognition, which enabled engineers servicing equipment to talk to and receive spoken answers from a computer that could recognize about 5,000 words. 1975 brought with it the IBM 5100 Portable Computer, a desktop that made computer capabilities more accessible to engineers, analysts, statisticians, and other problem solvers. At 50 pounds, it was a far cry from the ultraportable, four-pound or less systems we have today. We've come a long way, baby.

Apple computers came on the scene around this time. The company, Apple Computer, formed in 1976 with the idea of bringing computer power to ordinary people with ordinary budgets. The first machine had few features; most notable was the use of a television as the display. Many machines at the time had no display.

The early model Apple computer
Image courtesy of Steve Jurvetson on Flickr

About 200 Apple I computers were built and circulated, and by 1977, Apple unveiled the Apple II. This model, along with the Commodore PET from Chuck Peddle and the TRS-80 from Tandy Corporation (later Radio Shack), became known as the "1977 Trinity." These three computers are generally credited with creating the home computer market. The Apple III was released in 1980, targeting the business market. This model struggled some initially, the design contained no internal cooling fan, and the units were prone to overheating. A new model was introduced in 1983, but damage was done to the brand's reputation.

IBM entered the personal computer market in 1981 with the IBM Personal Computer (PC), joining ranks with Apple, which was well established in the market. The IBM PC offered users a choice in operating systems. Most selected PC DOS (from Microsoft). By 1983, the PC surpassed the Apple II as the best-selling personal computer. In 1985, one of the Apple Computers founders, Steve Jobs, left the company. Technology users at this time generally found themselves in one of two camps: Mac (meaning Apple) or PC (meaning Microsoft). This standoff has continued to present day, although it has assumed increasingly less significance with the advent of web-based software.

IBM's ThinkPad debuted in 1992, becoming an instant hit. The company coined the term "e-business" in 1997, defining an industry that uses the Internet as a medium for real business. The term would become synonymous with doing business in the

Internet age. Around this same time, Jobs returned to Apple as interim chief executive officer and began a critical restructure of the company. That same year, Apple introduced the Apple Store as an online retail store (the brick-and-mortar stores you find across the country today started showing up in 2001).

Apple debuted the iMac in 1998, a move that bought Apple time to restructure. The system was a hit and ushered in a new era for Apple with an emphasis on the design and aesthetics of its products—an emphasis that continues to date. In 1999, Apple introduced the iBook, its first consumer-oriented laptop and the first Macintosh to support the use of a wireless local area network (LAN) (enabling the laptop to connect to the Internet wirelessly).

In 2001, Apple introduced the iPod, a portable digital audio player, and vast improvement to the Walkman (audiocassette player) and Discman (compact disc player). The iPod started as a five-gigabyte player that could store around 1,000 songs. The iPod was a huge success for Apple and in 2003, Apple launched the iTunes Music Store. In 2007, Apple unveiled the first version of the iPhone, a device that combined the wide screen from the iPod with the world's first mobile device offering an Internet communicator able to run Apple's web browser, Safari. This revolutionary technology prompted a resurgence for Apple. On May 26, 2010, Apple's stock market value overtook Microsoft's value.

During this time of rapid technological evolution, people again divided into two camps (Mac or PC), with each having a cult following of sorts. The distinction is almost negligible in today's age, the era of the cloud. Hardware and software alike are designed to work with browser-based applications, with little to no notice of whether you are working from a Mac or PC. The cloud has similarly whittled away the distinctions between Android and iPhone users.

This historical survey drives home the point that change is happening constantly and quickly. We are here to offer tips on how to harness the power behind this technology and to embrace and adapt to the changes as they occur. Technology is here to help you, and we are too.

OFFICE TECHNOLOGY

SET UP A WI-FI NETWORK IN YOUR OFFICE

Setting up a network involves purchasing Internet access through a provider. Such providers use a variety of means of connection, ranging from hard-wired connections to cable connections to wireless connections using satellites. You will also need to obtain a Wi-Fi router with the ability to set wired and wireless (or just wireless) networks. You can easily find decent Wi-Fi routers through Amazon.com, or at Best Buy, Fry's, Costco, or just about anywhere else that they sell modern electronic equipment. Brands to look for include Linksys, Netgear, and D-Link.

If you do not already have connectivity with the Internet service provider (ISP) you plan to use, give some serious thought to where you locate the primary connection to the provider's equipment. That will be the spot where, most likely, you will put your principal equipment (modem/router) for connectivity. You want a clear signal to go throughout your building to everywhere you will want or need connectivity. You greatly increase the likelihood of accomplishing that if you keep your equipment away from potentially conflicting signals (i.e., other routers or electrical equipment) and away from substantial walls and/or furniture that might block or impair the signal's ability to move through the building. If you will want connectivity on more than one floor, you will do best with your router on a higher floor than a lower one. Coverage of the lower floor from a router on the higher floor generally works easier and better than trying to get coverage on the upper floor from a router on the main floor.

Connect the router to your broadband network and follow the directions provided with the router to access the router and set up the network. Give the network a name (preferably not your name, your office's name, or your office's address) and passwords. Most routers will want two passwords, one for administrative access and the other for general use. Use strong passwords for both to protect access and the confidentiality of your data. A strong password includes alphabetical (upper and lower case), numeric, and symbolic characters, does not tie closely to you (i.e., not your birthday or address, and so on), and contains at least eight characters. Longer is better. A good example of a strong password is "bEwArE#ThE#jAbBeRwOcK$666." Random combination passwords offer the most strength; but they also create the most difficulty to remember. You can get software that will generate and store random character passwords for you.

Do NOT give out the administrative password to anyone other than a trusted employee or information technology (IT) person with administrative responsibility for your network. In a small office, you may do your own IT work. In that case, you will want to have a copy of the password accessible to someone else for emergency situations. You could provide the Internet access password for your office network to everyone in your office who will connect to it. A better alternative is to connect them yourself and lock the password in a safe place where you could provide it to others in an emergency. If they already have the network connection established and stored in their computers and/or mobile devices, they do not need the password, as its only function is to allow connectivity to appropriate personnel. The connection process has become easy. Usually the computer or mobile device will provide a list of the available networks it sees when you turn on wireless connectivity on the device. Select your network and it should ask for the password. Enter the password and the device should connect to the network. Once a device has connected to a network, most will automatically reconnect to the same network when available (note that with some devices you must go to the "Settings" menu and choose this option).

SET UP A GUEST WI-FI NETWORK IN YOUR OFFICE

For those of us who work outside of our physical offices frequently, the availability of Wi-Fi makes our lives much easier. What we can do without Internet access looks very limited by comparison to what Internet access enables us to accomplish. Having Internet access available to us almost everywhere has become commonplace. Many, if not most, law offices now have courtesy Wi-Fi available for guests.

The flip side of using Internet access that you may find in another attorney's office is that when other attorneys (and sometimes clients) come to your office, they may want to use the Internet. When that happens, you have three choices: (1) you can tell them you do not have guest Internet access; (2) you can allow them to access the Internet using the same network you use for your office; or (3) you can provide a guest network to them (which operates separately from your main office network). Of those options, number two is really "number two." Stay away from it, as it needlessly exposes your network and confidential data. The first listed option leaves your data protected; but clients, guests, and other attorneys may see it as an inconvenience. Number three provides the best option. It costs you virtually nothing, it keeps your data protected by keeping outsiders off of your main network, and it provides Internet access to guests, clients, and other attorneys as a courtesy.

Setting up a guest network involves purchasing a Wi-Fi router capable of handling two or more networks (if you do not already have one). You can easily find two or more network Wi-Fi routers through Amazon.com, Best Buy, Fry's, Costco, or just about anywhere else selling modern electronic equipment. If you already have a good single-band router and do not want to buy a dual-band (or multiple-band) router, you have the option of adding a second single-band router to your equipment. As a practical matter, the routers keep getting better, so you may get a better network from the newer router and, for that reason, replacing an older single-band router with a newer two-band or multi-band router makes good sense. You can find excellent dual-band routers for between $100 and $250. You can find single-band routers for as little as $25, but the faster, better ones are in the range of $80 and up. If you have a good, fast, single-band router and do not want to upgrade to a dual-band router, you might think about picking up a mid-range ($40–$50) single-band router for the guest network. Brands to look for include Linksys, Netgear, and D-Link. If you go with two routers, try to position the routers as far away from each other as you can to reduce the risk that they will interfere with each other.

Connect the new router to your broad-band network and follow the directions to access the router and set up the networks. Give them different names and different passwords. Use strong passwords for both (you might as well keep strangers from using it without your permission). Note that you will likely want two passwords for each, one for administrative access and the other for Internet access. Make both strong. (See "Set Up a Wi-Fi Network in Your Office" for information about strong passwords.)

Follow the same protocols for the administrative password to the guest network as you do with respect to your primary office network. Even though you will not have your confidential information on the guest network, you do not want to lose control.

Regarding the guest network, while you could connect everyone yourself, that imposes an unnecessary burden on you and your time. No good reason exists to do that as opposed to providing the guest network user with the password. In many offices, there are access instructions provided in printed form to visitors. That saves a lot of time for your staff. Even though the guest network may use the same Internet provider and initial access point and emanate from the same router as your office network, it does not connect to your office network, keeping your office information secure. To ensure the protection of your confidential information, stay off of the guest network and do not access it or allow any access to it from computers on your primary office network, as those computers likely will contain confidential information that could become compromised. You will want to change your guest network's password relatively frequently (at least once every month or two) to minimize the risk of the password getting out and allowing unwelcome strangers to access it and get free Internet at your expense. Besides, if too many users jump onto your network, it will likely slow down the network's operations.

TROUBLESHOOTING YOUR WI-FI NETWORK

Step 1 : **CHECK YOUR CONNECTIONS.** If you cannot connect a device to your network or cannot get through to the Internet, start by checking your connections. Make sure that all of the required connections to the router are in place and proper. If you find a loose or unreliable connection, replace the connecting cable, restart, and see if that solves the problem. Often it will. If it does not, then go to Step 2.

Step 2: CHECK YOUR SETTINGS. Make sure you have turned on the Wi-Fi setting on your device(s). Also make sure you have selected the correct network and properly entered the network's password. If you set up the network without a password, you will not need to worry about entering a password; but neither will anyone else. We recommend that you fix that immediately and put a secure (strong) password in place. While you can set most devices to automatically reconnect to a network to which they have previously connected, sometimes that does not work. Sometimes a system update or another event changes your setting. Because of that, you will want to make sure they match your expectations and the network's requirements. Try reentering your password. If all appears in order, try telling your device to forget that network (meaning it will not automatically reconnect) and then reconnect manually (if that works, and you have your device set to remember networks to which it attaches, it will reconnect automatically going forward).

Step 3: TURN IT OFF; TURN IT ALL OFF! This is as basic as it gets, but it solves many problems. We start by rebooting our device to see if that solves the problem. If it does not, we move to a more involved procedure. Power down the devices you are connecting to the network and then power down the network itself by turning off the router and the modem you use to connect to the Internet. If you have more devices plugged into your router, power them all down. Even if the device has a power switch (not all do), pull the plug. While it works if you pull the plug out of the wall socket or the connector out of the device, we recommend the former over the latter. We make that recommendation because if you unplug the connector from the device and mix up the connectors when you reconnect you might fry one or more of your devices (or it might just not work). If you unplug from the wall, you cannot screw up the reconnection without work-ing very hard at it. If you choose to pull the connectors from the devices, first mark the wires to ensure that you do not plug a power block into the wrong device; it may not work and you could fry the device (not all power blocks produce the same output, even if they have similar connectors). Similarly, not all devices accept the same level of power input. After you pull the plug on everything, wait a minute and then start reconnecting devices to the power source, exercising caution to ensure that you plug the right power connector to each device. When you reconnect, start with the device closest to the Internet and proceed one by one, until you get to the devices you will connect to the network. Ideally, you will have the patience to wait until one device indicates it is live and connected to the Internet before powering up the next one. Once you have your network up and running again, you should be able to power up your devices and connect them to the network.

Step 4: LOCATION, LOCATION, LOCATION. If you have a weak or intermittent connectivity at certain locations, you can improve network performance by relocating the router or your device. This process requires you to experiment with different positions to find the situation that works best for you. As your router will likely have to remain fairly close to your primary Internet connection, moving the connecting devices may prove the easiest to accomplish. If your network performance reflects intermittent problems look for other wireless routers and electrical devices that could generate interference (fans, microwave ovens, and so on) and try to keep them as far away from the router as possible. Try to make sure that the router is at least three feet away from other signal-generating devices. Note that these days it may not be unusual to have multiple networks served by multiple routers. Additionally, most offices have other electronic equipment that can generate interfering signals (such as microwave ovens).

Step 5: CHANGE YOUR SIGNAL. If you discover interference but cannot move your equipment far enough from the interference to stop it, try changing the channel on which your router operates (if you have multiple systems that are not connected devices (e.g., a wireless router for your network and a separate router for a wireless alarm system), you want to make sure that each operates on a different channel). You can also try switching the frequency, if you have a router that operates on more than one frequency (2.4 gigahertz [GHz] and 5.0 GHz are the two most common). Consider different channels and frequencies in connection with any relocation of the router or your connecting devices, as different frequencies and channels may perform differently at the same location.

Step 6: GIVE YOUR NETWORK A BOOST. If you still have connection problems after going through the procedures suggested in Steps 1–4, you may have a dead spot in your network. A dead spot means you get little or no wireless signal to your devices in certain locations. If you have that problem and cannot solve it using the process in Step 4, consider adding a piece of equipment called a repeater (sometimes also called a signal booster or a range extender). These devices (usually around $50) get set up solidly within the range of the primary router's strongest signal area, but between the primary router and the dead spot. They receive and rebroadcast the signal from the router. If set up in a proper location, they can create or increase the signal to your dead spot. Some vendors of the newer routers have come out with a group of interconnected devices that they sell as a single package. The devices rebroadcast the signal to ensure better coverage for the network throughout your building.

USING WI-FI TO SAFELY CONNECT TO THE INTERNET

In a quarter of a century, the Internet evolved from an esoteric academic repository of information to a primary means of storage and communication of information in our society affecting our personal and our professional lives. We learned that we could transmit vast quantities of information over great distances in short time periods through the Internet. Having made that discovery, we have grown increasingly dependent on the Internet as a primary means of communications with and connection to our friends, our colleagues, our offices, and our information.

Through the Internet, we can transmit execution copies of documents almost instantly to people all over the world. People can sign the documents electronically and return them immediately. The Internet's utility goes far beyond documents. We can transmit audio tracks such as radio broadcasts, music, and so on. We can transmit pictures in still format or even video across great distances almost instantaneously. The Internet has grown in use and utility to where news broadcasts can occur online, we can hold live videoconferences online, and we can take college courses online. Voice over Internet Protocol (VoIP) allows us to use the Internet for inexpensive telephonic communications.

The increased use of and dependence on the Internet continues to drive the development of faster and faster transmission and retrieval speeds for Internet connectivity.

As the power and speed of laptop computers increased and the cost of portability decreased, more and more of us gravitated towards the use of laptop computers either to supplement desktop models or as a complete replacement in some cases.

The recent evolution of wireless connectivity has also increased the appeal and the use of laptop computers and other wireless devices, such as tablets and smartphones. Through wireless connectivity, we can have fast Internet access in many locations where it was not previously feasible to do so. We can move devices around our homes and our offices to suit our convenience while maintaining high-speed

Internet access and connectivity, without the need of a hard-wired connection, by installing a wireless router or access point. Ease of connection grew paramount, so that "everyone" could use wireless connectivity. Software and hardware evolved to where now you do not have to do much more than turn the computer on and let its operating system negotiate the connection issues for you.

For those of us who frequently work outside of our physical offices, the availability of Wi-Fi makes our lives much easier. What we can do without Internet access looks very limited by comparison to what we can do with Internet access. Having Internet access available to us almost everywhere has become commonplace. Coffee shops, restaurants, hotels, other law offices, and many public areas frequently have Wi-Fi available. Historically, hotels have charged for Wi-Fi, but that model no longer dominates, and hotels often offer free Wi-Fi in lobbies and guest rooms. Generally, hotels still charge for access in conference rooms.

You can buy a cellular hotspot that will fit in your pocket and carry your own Internet access that works wherever you can get a cellular connection to your provider. Most providers have this available. While your domestic provider may have some international access available, cellular data tends to cost far more when your domestic provider sells access to you in another country. When traveling outside of the United States, if you will spend most of your time in an area serviced by a local provider, you will generally do better for telephone and data if you have an unlocked device and can purchase a Subscriber Identity Module (SIM) card and a data plan from that provider. We have also recently discovered some devices and providers designed specifically for international travel. These providers will sell you daily access to the Internet at a cost generally more than what you pay here, but less than you would pay your domestic provider for access in another country. The downside is that these providers generally use 3G systems that provide a considerably slower access than the 4G or Wi-Fi access you probably use most of the time.

Even if you have acquired one of these devices, you will likely find that the Wi-Fi available locally to you works faster and undoubtedly costs less. The downside of using it, however, is that it provides a far less secure connection than using your own controlled and secure hotspot. To minimize exposure and confidentiality issues resulting from the lower security offered by these public Wi-Fi connections, you will want to make sure that you use a virtual private network (VPN) to protect your communications. A VPN effectively provides you with a tunnel through cyberspace, insulating your communications and protecting them (and you) from general public access to your transmissions. You can set up your own VPN or use a commercial VPN. The commercial VPNs usually provide service to you on a subscription basis for a fee. You can easily find commercial VPNs and sign up for their service. There are several very good ones. VPN Unlimited has performed well consistently over the past few years. You can also set up your own VPN, if you have the technological know-how or an IT person who does.

HELP YOUR CLIENTS FEEL INVOLVED IN THEIR CASE WITH CLIENT PORTALS

A client portal is a web-accessible, secure website used for file sharing and storage. If you set up such a site, your client can use the same link every time to log in to his or her personal portal. You can ensure it always has the correct version of all files available for safe, secure access. Clients can see the status of documents relating to their matter 24/7 without you having to be available to answer their call.

Having a client portal can save you time and your client money by reducing the risk of lost attachments or e-mails accidentally deleted or sent to a spam folder. It is an easy way to make sure you both are looking at the latest version of a document when collaborating remotely. It is much more effective than exchanging e-mails back and forth and trying to remember whether you received or sent the latest version.

One easy way to set up client portals is through Citrix ShareFile. ShareFile allows you to add an unlimited number of client portals. It also offers security features you should be using like encrypted e-mail, e-signature software, desktop file sync, and the ability to transfer large file sizes (up to 100 gigabytes [GB]). Plans start at $16/month for a solo practitioner/single user (remember you can set up unlimited portals, though this is limited to 100 GB of storage total, 10 GB max file size), $60/month for five attorney/user accounts ($8/additional user, limited to 1 terabyte (TB) of storage total, 10 GB max file size), or for a document-intensive practice you may prefer the business plan at $100/month for five attorney/user accounts ($10/additional user, unlimited storage, 100 GB max file size).

To use ShareFile, your clients will need to have their own unique log-in credentials. We recommend you set this up at the beginning of your professional relationship by incorporating guidelines for technology use and securely exchanging information in your client engagement letter. Your client will need to hang on to the access credentials (username and password). Every time you send a secure e-mail or file to the client, he or she will be alerted via e-mail and instructed how to access the file. The client will then be required to log in and then he or she will be given a secure link to view or download the file.

Setting up a client portal in ShareFile is easy. Once you have the software set up, you simply:

1. Identify the folders and files you would like your clients to access
2. Define client profiles, sharing rules, and roles
3. Customize the portal with your logo, for a personal and professional touch

If you are concerned that clients will find this technology cumbersome, most clients find it simple and intuitive to use. They also enjoy being able to send and receive documents without driving in or to discover the status of a matter without having to call and ask someone.

USE FREECONFERENCECALL.COM TO GET FREE CONFERENCE CALLS

A conference call is a telephone call in which several people can talk simultaneously. Conference calls may allow all the callers to participate during the call, or the call may be set up so certain callers can merely listen to the call and cannot speak (like webinars you may have called into). Conference calls can be designed so the calling party calls the other participants and adds them to the call; however, participants can usually call into the conference call themselves by dialing a telephone number that connects to a "conference bridge" (a specialized type of equipment that links telephone lines).

Businesses use conference calls regularly for collaboration with others remotely, client meetings or presentations, project meetings and updates, regular team meetings, training classes, and communication with colleagues who work in different locations. Conference calling is a way to cut travel costs and allow workers to be more productive by not having to go out-of-office for meetings.

If you need to set up a conference call and do not have this feature as part of your telephone service, check out FreeConfer enceCall.com. As the name suggests, Free ConferenceCall.com provides high-quality, high-definition (HD) audio conferencing, screen sharing, video conferencing, audio and visual recordings, customized greetings, security features, calendar integrations, and mobile applications.

To get started, go to https://www.free conferencecall.com/ and set up an account. Once you have created a username and password the service will assign you a conference call number (note, it is not toll-free, so long distance charges may apply). You will also get an access code and a host personal identification number (PIN). Document all this information so you can circulate it in an e-mail to your conference call participants.

You can invite people to the call by e-mailing them the call-in details (phone number, access code, and host PIN if you may not be the host). You can also invite

them from within the app using a Google calendar extension or a Microsoft Outlook plug-in. The number and code are unique to your account, so you will use the same PIN and phone number for future calls as well. At the scheduled time, everyone calls the dial-in number and enters the access code followed by pound or hash (#). If you are the host, enter the host PIN followed by pound or hash (#).

You can record the conference call if you are the host of the call. To do so, dial in as the host (call your dial-in number and enter the access code followed by pound or hash (#), then press star (*) and enter the host PIN when prompted). To record, press *9 and 1 to confirm. To stop and save the recording, press *9 again and 1 to confirm.

You can use the site to host an audio-only conference call or an online meeting, where call-in participants can view your screen during a call. This is a useful way to illustrate what you are saying or to show-case a PowerPoint presentation during the call.

To host an online meeting, download the desktop app. At the time of your call, open the desktop app and enter your user identification (e-mail) and password. You will then click "play" and select items to screen share. Lastly, click "camera" and select your audio preference to start video conferencing.

If you are worried about long distance charges applying (not everyone has free long distance calling), you can offer participants a toll-free number to call into; however, you will pay 3.9¢/minute for this service, so an hour-long call would cost you $2.34.

REMOTE CONFERENCE CALLS

Conference calls can be a useful collaboration tool or the bane of your workday, depending on how well your technology functions. To have the flexibility to conduct a conference call anywhere, you will want a conference phone that is rechargeable, wireless, and able to connect to a cell phone via Bluetooth. Other important factors in choosing a conference call speakerphone include:

1. Room size—Conference phones have different microphone pickup ranges. You will want to know how big the room will be and how far from the speaker you can get and still be heard.
2. Clarity
3. Sound quality
4. Power supply—Whether it requires access to a power outlet or can connect to a computer or run wirelessly or with batteries
5. Call recording—Some models come with call recording features; this

can be useful if you want to review important details or share the call with a colleague.

6. Effectiveness at reducing background noise

Often, people prefer a conference phone be connected to a traditional analog landline rather than a cell phone or VoIP service, but sometimes this option is not available. The other big complaint is having two people talking at once, but you cannot always stop this from happening if you were all in the same room; so, not surprisingly, it happens over conference calls as well.

If you are in the market for a speakerphone for your conference room, or one you can take when you travel, try these:

Model:	Cost (in USD, as of 2018):	Available at:	Why we like it:
Logitech P710e	$155.06	Amazon .com	Great sound quality, good for small conference rooms with up to ten people

Model:	Cost (in USD, as of 2018):	Available at:	Why we like it:
Harman Kardon Esquire Mini Gold Portable Bluetooth Speaker w/ Speakerphone	$69.95	Walmart.com	Great sound quality, customizable colors, lightweight, slim profile
Konftel EGO Personal Portable Bluetooth Conferencing Unit	$96.00	Amazon.com	Lightweight, great omni-sound audio quality

If you find yourself responsible for setting up a conference call, here are a few tips to help you:

1. **Know your technology before the call begins**. You do not want the call to start before you learn how to use the audio equipment. Practice ahead of time to make sure everything works as it was intended. This will allow you to test your signal strength if you are planning to connect via a cell phone or Internet connection.

2. **Try to keep the ambient noise level low**. Hopefully your conference room is surrounded by solid walls that inhibit you from hearing what is going on next door. Try to avoid rooms with noisy air conditioners or open windows. Silence all cell phones in the room and avoid flipping through pages of paper.

3. **Use a speakerphone with 360° microphones to capture people speaking from all sides**. If your device does not have surrounding microphones, then designate a seat for speakers to move to so the callers not in the room can hear them.

Follow these tips and you will be handling conference calls with remote attendees like a pro.

AI TECHNOLOGY AND ROSS

It seems every few years, people buzz about artificial intelligence (AI) and robot lawyers. You may have even heard of IBM's Watson and the cognitive computing model. Watson is IBM's supercomputer that competed on the television show *Jeopardy!* and won. Merriam-Webster defines AI as "an area of computer science that deals with giving machines the ability to seem like they have human intelligence" and "the capability of a machine to imitate intelligent human behavior" (https://www.merriam-webster.com/dictionary/artificial%20intelligence). Have no fear though; despite rapid and revolutionary advancement, machines have not developed the ability to replace a skilled lawyer, and most likely never will. However, the advancements here now can make practicing law more efficient and effective.

So, who is ROSS, or what is it?

ROSS is an artificially intelligent legal research system that gets smarter each day you use it. The engine that powers ROSS, Legal Cognition, is what allows

Photo by Daniil Kuželev on Unsplash

ROSS to read legal texts and recognize and answer complex research questions. ROSS searches through a vast legal database to rapidly answer any legal question. You can ask ROSS legal questions in natural language, like you would ask another lawyer in conversation. ROSS runs in the cloud and is easy and fast to set up. It is intuitive and requires little training. In 2016, one of the country's biggest law firms, Baker Hostetler, became one of the first firms to hire the "robot lawyer" as a legal researcher for their bankruptcy division. The small law firm Salazar Jackson, in Florida, also employs ROSS's services, rationalizing that the service costs less than it would cost to hire a junior associate. Now the firm starts their legal research with ROSS, and if their attorneys need to they can go deeper. Founding partner Luis Salazar has found ROSS's response to be about the same as he could do, even with his 20 years of experience.

You may be asking yourself, how does this relate to me and my practice? For starters, if you find yourself in one of the firms adopting ROSS or similar AI technology, we want you to understand it better in hopes it will assist you in adopting it. Also, we want you to be aware of this developing change because it can lead to tools that make your practice more efficient and enable you to practice longer.

MULTI-FUNCTION KEYBOARDS

Whether you are working or playing around with a hobby, the keyboard is an integral part of your office setup. Most people do not give a second thought to their keyboard, until a key pops off or gets stuck in a way that renders it useless. It is perhaps the most hands-on interface of your computer, and sometimes for tablets too. Considering all this, it is worth taking a moment to look at what keyboard options are out there, and a few we particularly like.

Some factors to consider when choosing a keyboard include:

Connectivity Options. This pertains to how your keyboard connects to your device. Generally, the options out there are via Universal Serial Bus (USB), wireless, or Bluetooth. Choosing between these options is more of a personal preference. If your device is mostly stationary (like a desktop computer), you might consider a wired connection or wireless. A wired connection is powered by your personal computer (PC), so you do not have to worry about recharging your keyboard or changing the batteries (a plus). You do have to put up with being tethered to your desktop tower, and the cluttered look of the cord attached to it (a negative.) If you want more freedom to rearrange your desktop configuration and less cord clutter, look to a wireless keyboard. If your device is mobile, or if you prefer to move about in different configurations for comfort, consider the wireless or Bluetooth connection keyboards.

Layout and Ergonomics. This pertains to the physical design of the keyboard, the key layout, and materials. As standard as a keyboard is to a computer, the design of the keyboard is hardly so standardized. For instance, only around half the keyboards on the market come with the ten-key numeric pad for fast calculations and number entry. Most keyboards also contain keys for volume and playback control. Many keyboards can modify the angle of the keys to keep your hands in a neutral position, easing carpal tunnel and repetitive stress syndromes. These modifications not only improve comfort, but reduce stress to the joints and tendons, ultimately helping you to avoid painful inflammation and expensive surgery. Ergonomic features can range from simple modifications, like padded wrist rests, to elaborate keyboards that curve and slope.

The Logitech Bluetooth Easy-Switch Keyboard is specifically designed for Mac users and will not work with PC computers. It bears the name "Easy-Switch" because you can connect your Mac, iPhone, iPad, or Apple TV to it and easily switch from typing on one to any of the others. The F1, F2, and F3 keys are the activators to switch between each device, depending on the order in which you pair it. This means with the stroke of a key you can go from typing up notes on your Mac to replying to a text message on your iPhone, all from the convenience of your keyboard. The design of the keyboard features bright backlit keys, which allow for improved typing in poor light conditions. The keys are a comfortable size for typing, with a chiclet-style rounded square shape that is whisper-quiet while you are working. The keys' smooth finish feels nice while typing. Many users report their typing speed is faster with the keyboard because of how comfortable it feels, compared to Apple's standard desktop keyboard. Like most Mac products, the keyboard has a sleek, smooth design, and is shiny and minimal. One drawback to that minimal design worth noting is the absence of the ten-key number pad. This is a rechargeable, wireless keyboard. It recharges via a USB cable you can connect and continue working while it is charging. The wireless connectivity works at a range up to 33 feet.

If you are a fan of the original IBM Model M Keyboard, you will likely enjoy the Unicomp Ultra Classic Model M black keyboard. This keyboard is lauded as providing the most comfortable typing experience, which is handy if you type a great deal. The biggest complaint is that it is loud, sounding more like traditional typewriting than the whisper-quiet features of the Logitech Easy-Switch. This is largely due to the buckling spring underlying each key. Unicomp purchased the design of the Model M keyboard from IBM and has stayed true to the original model. The keys are large, and very responsive to touch. The keyboard comes with two pop-out feet to adjust the angle of the board. In addition to the traditional models you can buy on Amazon .com, for a $10 fee, you can custom design your own keyboard with any of 34 languages and layouts (including variations of Dvorak, Mac, and Linux, and blank keycaps are an option). Numerous other styles can also be purchased at varying prices. All the keyboards are made at Unicomp's facilities in Lexington, Kentucky.

Another popular choice is Logitech's Wireless Wave keyboard. This keyboard is rated high for comfort, design, and functionality. The wireless connectivity is nice for keeping your desktop free from cord clutter and the key layouts include multitasking hot keys like audio-playback and keys on the left side to zoom in (helpful for aging eyes), and hot keys to open photos or music players. The ergonomic wave design provides a more comfortable typing experience, and the built-in padded wrist rest helps ease repetitive stress syndrome, as mentioned earlier. The keys offer a mechanical/silicone key switch hybrid as a sort of middle ground between the other two keyboards. As a wireless keyboard, it is battery operated, but the battery life is exceptional, with keyboards lasting up to three years before needing new batteries.

VISUAL AIDS FOR YOUR TECHNOLOGY

Most seniors can attest that with aging, your hearing, dexterity, and eyesight decline. This can make using a smartphone more difficult. You do not want to squint to read the tiny font or keypad. Some smartphone manufacturers have alleviated this with larger phone screens. For example, the iPhone 7 Plus from Apple boasts a sizable 5.5-inch screen and allows you to adjust the text size and the background light for easier reading. The LG G6 offers a 5.7-inch display and is powered by Google Assistant, the same software that powers the Google Home. This allows you to set up appointments and get reminders.

The Samsung Galaxy S8 has a 6.2-inch screen and can be set to run in easy mode, which gives the phone a simpler layout, less distracting features, and larger fonts that may work better for tired eyes. The Android operating system on the Galaxy S8 also offers TalkBack, an accessibility setting that helps vision-impaired users enjoy their devices. With TalkBack enabled, you can use spoken-word commands and receive vibration and audible feedback to let you know what is on your screen, what you are touching, and what you can do with it.

In addition to adjusting phone settings, tools can help you while using a smartphone. For instance, you can get a smartphone screen magnifier to make watching shows and reading on your smartphone easier. The Dizaul Screen Magnifier ($14.95, Amazon.com) is often recommended for offering HD magnification. This is a low-tech tool, requiring no power supply, and generally works with all smartphones. Enlarging the screen eases eye strain and fatigue. You cannot communicate with the device through the screen, but it is handy for watching videos. The display folds up with a slim profile, making it easy to travel with. You can also adjust the viewing angle for comfort.

If you are feeling nostalgic, you might like the Retro TV Smartphone Magnifier from Urban Outfitters ($19.99, UrbanOut fitters.com), another low-tech device that will magnify the screen. Your grandkids might get a kick out of watching television the way you did as a kid (sort of).

Littleton Coin Company has the Phonescope Magnifier ($25.95, LittletonCoin.com) that clips onto your phone, over the camera lens, and magnifies the image up to 60 times. You can use this to see a lot of detail on your display, and even take pictures with it. It is a handy tool for reading small print if you encounter that a lot when you are out.

MaxiAids, a company that provides several lifestyle assistance tools, has the Portable Small Screen Magnifier ($69.99, Amazon.com) that you can use for easier reading while typing a message on your smartphone. The title reads for iPods or Blackberry devices, but the design is such it would work on any smartphone.

PICK THE TIME YOU SEND YOUR E-MAIL

Over the years, we have had several people ask us about writing e-mails at one time and sending them at another. The easiest way we have found to do that works in Microsoft Outlook. The good news is that it works both on the current Mac and on the Windows versions of Outlook. For those of you who use both platforms, the bad news is that you have to remember two different sets of steps. Fortunately, you can do it fairly easily on either platform.

On the Mac, open an e-mail message and when you enter the address of the recipient, if you are in the "Message" tab, you will see that the send button in the top left-hand corner of the message window lights up to allow you to push the button and send it. To the right of the button you will see a small arrow pointing down. If you click that arrow it will open a box that will allow you to choose a later date and time to send the e-mail. Outlook will hold the e-mail in your outbox until the chosen date and time and then release it.

On the Windows platform, click the "Options" tab and go to the "Delay Delivery" button on the right side near the top. You click on that and select the date and time of delivery and Outlook holds the mail in your outbox until the chosen date and time; then it releases it for transmittal.

Unfortunately for Mac users, Apple's Mail program does not have this feature, so you cannot delay e-mails and have them automatically sent at a preordained time and date. You can delay a completed e-mail, but you have to do it manually. To do that, simply click the red button in the top left corner after you have finished composing the message and before you hit send. That will cause a pop up to give you the choice of saving the message as a draft, not saving it, or canceling the instruction to close the box. If you select "Save," the message will sit in your outbox as a draft until you open it and manually hit the send button, shipping it off to your designated recipient(s).

BEAT THE COLD COFFEE BLUES WITH A USB COFFEE WARMER

Coffee, by itself, is a generally healthy way to wake up and get started in the morning. It is loaded with antioxidants and beneficial nutrients (absent the heavy creams, sugars, and alcohols people sometimes add). According to Healthline, a privately owned health information provider, the caffeine in coffee can help you feel less tired and increase energy levels, along with improving memory, mood, vigilance, reaction time, and general cognitive function. It can increase blood pressure, which may make it off limits for some, but those without high blood pressure concerns can benefit from a cup or two.

It is evident from the mass of coffee shops that most people are already on board with the health benefits of coffee. In 2012, U.S. workers spent an average of $3,000 a year on coffee. How often have you poured the remainder of your cup out after it went cold? Not to mention the time you spent making a fresh cup (a small amount initially but everything adds up over time.) This little trick can spare you wasting time and money. Pick up an electric mug warmer. They make warmers that plug into an outlet, or your computer via a USB connection (so you can keep your mug warm if you are working on a laptop at the park).

For $7, you can pick up a Mr. Coffee Electric Mug Warmer from Amazon.com. The warmer is a little over five inches wide, which is plenty of room for a ceramic mug. It even works with a small soup bowl if you are powering through lunch. The small black disc is functional at a great price. For a prettier warmer, consider the Norpro Decorative Mug Warmer ($17.27, Amazon .com). The little heater features a crackled marble design, although the heating surface area is smaller and better suited for coffee mugs. SimplyCoffee offers a USB warmer that works for coffee mugs, tea, soup, and wax candles. Although you may want to move the warmer to a different location if you switch from coffee to a wax candle, for we would not want you to forget and sip the wrong one.

If you find yourself on the road a lot, visiting clients, you may benefit from the AutoCafe Take-Out Hot Cup Warmer. This gadget is labeled as safe for disposable cups, similarly shaped porcelain travel mugs, Styrofoam, plastic, and metal cups. It comes with a 12-volt direct current (DC) plug and cord to connect to your car through the cigarette lighter and will automatically turn on when a cup is inserted and shut off when the cup is removed.

If you are into having your coffee or tea at the just right temperature, you might like the Ember Temperature Control Ceramic Mug ($79.99, Ember.com). This mug comes with a warmer built in and connects to a smartphone app where you can dictate the exact temperature at which you want the beverage to stay. The mug was named the winner of *TIME Magazine*'s Best Inventions of 2017 (evidencing just how seriously we take our coffee).

TURN YOUR USB PORTS INTO MULTI-TASKERS WITH A HUB

Common USB cable: the top end is called a "micro-USB" connection and the bottom end is a USB connector

For starters, USB is a common connection used to power devices and transmit data. USB generally refers to a type of cable connection used to transmit data or power across a short distance. A significant number of everyday hardware (including smartphones, e-Readers, tablets, thumb drives, external hard drives, mice, and so on) connect to computers via the USB port, making your computer ports precious real estate. Increasing the supply of that real estate is pretty easy with this hack, making your life a little easier and convenient. Adding one of these hubs to your desk area or conference rooms provides easy and convenient access to plug in the many devices people have. There are a few ways you can set up the hub, depending on how much effort you want to put in.

Not all USB hubs are created equal, and the right one for you will depend on your personal preference. Some hubs can transmit data between the connected device and a computer to which it is connected, and some hubs will only transmit power to recharge a device. Know what you want the hub to do and choose accordingly.

The easiest one to set up and get started is one that sits on your desktop. You can go with a low profile, no-frills solution or you can let a little personality in. The sky is the

Sample thumb drive plugged into a USB port of the computer

limit. For simplicity, try the Anker 10-Port USB Data Hub ($49.99, Amazon.com). Anker has a strong reputation for charging USB devices. Another great choice is the Plugable USB3-HUB7-81X 7-Port Powered USB 3.0 Hub ($24.95, Amazon.com). If you are providing this convenience in a conference room (or if you want to be really popular at the next conference you attend), pick up the SmartDelux Powered USB Hub ($69.99, Amazon.com). It features ten high-speed USB ports plus three additional "smart" charging ports, allowing for a fast charge even when all the other ports are in use.

For those who cannot bear the sight of cables, there are a few hubs designed to fit into your desk, keeping your surface clutter free. Some desks come with a pre-cut circular hole (around 2.5 inches, called a grommet hole) for running cables under the desk. If you have one of these there are several hubs you can set in there. Check out the Sedna USB 3.1 Gen 1 3-Port Hub ($47.90, Amazon.com). This hub connects to your computer, powers your devices, and can transfer data up to 5 GB/second.

If you have no predrilled grommet hole in your desk, you can mount a USB hub under your desk. Look at the COZOO Under Desk Headset Holder Mount ($22.99, Amazon .com), which features three USB charging ports, and Apple Watch Stand and earphone/headphone hanger hooks.

There are tons of USB hubs of all shapes and sizes, with varying numbers of ports. You can show your sense of humor with a banana-shaped USB hub (eBerry Plug and Play Creative Banana Style 4-Port High Speed USB Hub, $9.99, Amazon.com) or let R2-D2 from *Star Wars* sit on your desk and charge your devices (Star Wars R2-D2 USB 3.0 Charging Hub, $59.99, Think Geek.com). For a touch of nostalgia, you could use the Battleship hub made by Kikkerland ($93.23, ThisIsWhyImBroke.com).

MANAGE CORD CLUTTER

Cord clutter builds up over time and after years of practice (or just life in general) it can get overwhelming. One of the authors, Jeff, battled cord clutter head-on when, after 43 years, he closed his physical office and moved to practicing part-time from his home, along with a virtual office setup that gives him a place to collect mail and packages, meet with clients, and have an office address other than his house. In the process of preparing his home workspace, he discovered that some bad habits had created a morass of wires and cables that had no function but cluttered things up and made his work space less usable—and potentially interfered with the performance of some of the other technology. As authors, we want to help with some tips for managing the clutter in your work or home:

For starters, get rid of useless equipment. Sometimes we keep old and outdated hardware, even after we stop using it. Consider donating older technology to

schools and other charitable organizations. If equipment is broken beyond repair, make sure it gets to an appropriate disposal facility.

Get rid of useless cables. Removing equipment helps the situation, but you help it more if you remove all associated cables at the same time. It is tempting to hold onto a cable in case another device uses it, and if you do, take the time to "reel" or fold it into a storable configuration. It may help to contain it in a Ziploc bag and label the type of connection outside the bag. This will make it easier to store and find when needed. If cables are damaged, kinked, or frayed, dispose of them at an appropriate facility.

Label your cables. Take a piece of tape and write on it what the cable connects to, then tape it to the cable. This way, if you must disconnect the cables, you can easily reconnect them properly. This is especially important respecting power cables. Not all power cables deliver the same output to the devices to which they attach. Power cables may have plugs enabling them to attach to multiple devices, some of which take more or less power than others. Connecting a low-output power supply to a high-need device will make it work badly or not allow it to work. Connecting a high-output power supply to a low-need device can fry the device.

Practice electrical safety. Many houses were designed and built long before the array of technology we have today. Most did not come with the number of plugs or capacity to safely manage having so many devices plugged into them. Consider

having an electrician install multi-plug outlets to your home or office to accommodate
the electronics you anticipate using. Some
multi-plug outlets even come with USB terminals to reduce the number of plugs you
need to use. Surge protectors are useful
and can convert one outlet to six or eight
outlets. You can string together surge protectors, but electricians will tell you they
do not recommend running such devices
together. To solve this, there are devices
with surge protection that will convert a
single outlet to accommodate 20 or more
plugs, such as the Bestten 24-Outlet Heavy
Duty Metal Power Strip with 15-Foot Ultra
Long Power Cord, or try the Tonbux Wi-Fi
Smart Power Strip Surge Protector.

**Keep your cords where you want them
with CableDrop.** CableDrops are rubberized, drop-shaped cable holders with adhe-
sive on the bottom, allowing you to arrange
your cables in a set configuration and keep
them in place.

These tips should help ease the clutter
and stress of having cables everywhere.

REDUCE BACKGROUND NOISE WHILE WORKING

Loud noises around the office are so commonplace that most people barely register them above a mild annoyance. But these subtle interruptions can disrupt your thought process or distract you, making completing even routine tasks take exponentially longer. The sound of a coffee pot brewing may make you want to get up and go to the restroom, or a colleague walking in may remind you of a question you meant to ask. Not to mention the dreaded building and road construction that pops up occasionally. Whatever the sort, the time lost adds up and can leave you feeling frustrated for not having done more with your day. If hearing these sounds distracts you, consider investing in a pair of noise-cancelling headphones to make focusing easier. Noise-cancelling headphones prevent unwanted sounds from reaching your ears, but they still allow you to hear the music, audio books, podcasts, or whatever else you might want to listen to during the day. You may be asking yourself, if noise is distracting how can music be helpful? Studies have found that music can be non-distracting and make routine tasks more bearable.[1] One study added that if music is too quiet or too loud it can harm your creativity. Rather, music should be kept to an ambient or moderate level (around 70 decibels).

You will see headsets advertised as noise-isolation or noise-cancellation, and the two function slightly differently. Noise-isolation is sometimes known as "passive noise control," and it works like earplugs, keeping the noise from getting into your ears. Compare that to noise-cancellation, which is more "active." Instead of simply blocking out sound waves, it generates a frequency 180 degrees out of sync with the incoming noise, effectively cancelling it out

---

1. J.G. Fox & E.D. Embrey, *Music—An Aid to Productivity*, 3.4 Applied Ergonomics 202–05 (1972), *available at* https://www.gwern.net/docs/music-distrac tion/1972-fox.pdf.

(hence the name). Most noise-cancellation headphones come at a cost, but it can be well worth it if you get even an hour more productivity out of it. Some nice models to consider include:

Model	Amazon Price	Description
Jabra Evolve 75	$279.00	High-quality sound, active noise canceling, and excellent accuracy when dictating
Sennheiser Momentum Wireless	$399.95	Excellent audio performance, comfortable ear pads, and a 22-hour battery life
Bose Soundlink	$229.00	Can be used wired/ wirelessly, excellent audio performance
Plantronics BackBeat Pro	$180.98	Pleasant design and solid audio performance
Parrot Zik 2.0	$110.00– $320.00	Sleek design, customizable smart-touch panel
AKG N60 NC	$169.00	Lightweight, great for traveling

USE A CHARGING STATION TO MAKE SURE YOUR TECHNOLOGY IS READY WHEN YOU ARE

Smartphones, tablets, wearable smartwatches, and fitness trackers—all of this technology has infiltrated our lives, and keeping everything charged up and ready to go when you are can be a headache. Every rechargeable device comes with a cord, and often a plug, multiplying the clutter associated with that device. Having a dedicated charging station not only allows you to keep your devices recharged, it also allows you to create a routine of putting those devices in the same place every day, giving you a visual reminder at the end of the day if something is not in its place. You could just get a multi-outlet power strip, but you will still see all the bulky plugs and messy cables running around. Instead, consider getting a charging station (or make one yourself if you are feeling crafty). For the less crafty, you can find many charging stations out there to work with your technology. Some accommodate smartphones, tablets, watches, and many other devices. Here are a few we like:

MobileVision Bamboo 10-Port Charging Station. This version of the MobileVision charging station is one of the largest bamboo charging stations on the market. It will look right at home in your kitchen and can serve as a central point for charging devices when family and friends come over. It is available direct from https://www.mobile visionus.com/ for $89.95, or for $59.95 at Walmart.com.

Griffin's Cove USB Charging Station or the Power Dock Pro. The Cove ($149.99, Amazon.com) is a recharging station that features a clean and contemporary design. It can charge up to five tablets and smartphones and store them out of sight while they charge. Inside the station you will find easy-access shelves with a sliding door that hides your devices or can double as a handy tablet stand. It looks like it could blend in well in your kitchen or living room. The Power Dock Pro ($129.95, Amazon.com) can charge up to five devices, though it appears sleek and more space-aged than its demure counterpart. It provides up to 12 watts of charging power for each bay, allowing up to five tablets to be charged simultaneously.

You might also consider creating a charging station in the middle of your conference room for clients or guests to use with the Little Big Premium USB Charger ($22.49, Amazon.com), or something similar. It is an easy hack that guests and clients will appreciate. Users of the Little Big charger report that even with devices plugged into all the ports, everything still charges as fast as it would if plugged into a

single port. If you are in a rush to recharge, one port features a cutting-edge Qualcomm QC 3.0 quick charge connection.

GREEN OFFICE TECHNOLOGY— TECHNOLOGY SAVINGS

It is never too late to make positive changes for the environment. Some changes can have a positive impact on your wallet. "Greening" your practice or "going green" simply refers to implementing eco-friendly measures in your office to reduce waste and energy consumption. There are some simple measures you can take to get started:

1. **Reduce the electricity you use.** Develop a habit of turning off your computers, printers, and any equipment that need not be left on at the end of the day. Leave them off until you need to use them again. This does not apply to things like network servers, fax machines, or your Internet routers that need to be on to send and receive data. When your light bulbs burn out you can replace them with energy-efficient bulbs. If you replaced the five most frequently used light fixtures with Energy Star efficient bulbs you can

quickly realize up to $75 in savings a year (which easily offsets the cost of energy-efficient bulbs).

2. **Recycle more**. Recycling can be as easy as picking up one of those blue recycle bins (if your office building employs such a service) for discarding paper. You can go further by encouraging staff to use their own cups rather than paper or Styrofoam cups, though we understand keeping these around for visitors. Identify local stores that will recycle your electronics (and remember to wipe the hard drives if anything contains personal or confidential data). If enough people employ these simple measures, it makes a difference.

3. **Telecommuting**. One way to improve the environmental friendliness of your office is to encourage working from home, particularly if you live in an area where most of your workers drive to work.

4. **Transportation choices**. For staff that have to drive in, you can

encourage carpooling or use of public transportation where possible.

5. **Consider a casual dress code in warmer months**. Not having to wear suits to the office can help reduce cooling costs during the warm summer months.

This list is not exhaustive, and you can pick and choose which ones you would consider trying. Every little bit helps and some of these measures will save you money, creating a win-win situation.

SLACK OFFICE COMMUNICATIONS

Slack is a cloud-based set of team collaboration tools and services for the office. Most commonly it is called a messaging application for teams. Beyond that, Slack integrates numerous platforms into one location. What does this mean for you? As lawyers, our professional lives are spread across numerous platforms. E-mail platforms, practice management platforms, document control systems, and timekeeping and billing platforms are just a few of the more common examples.

Some benefits of Slack include:

1. Messages can be exchanged instantaneously, encouraging collaboration between team members, unlike e-mail, which can have significant lag time.
2. Slack is very searchable.
3. Using Slack for those "quick questions" reduces the clutter in your e-mail inbox.

While these benefits sound great, there are a few drawbacks. For one, incorporating a system like Slack into your workflow creates yet another thing to keep track of and manage, adding to the pile of e-mails, voicemails, and written correspondence.

However, if you struggle to manage your communications, this could be a very useful tool for you to unify them with. As an added benefit, if you do not currently have a client portal set up, you can create a client portal using Slack. Slack offers the features you would expect a client portal to have—messaging, notifications, file uploads, and storage. You create a client portal by creating a channel, which in Slack terminology is a chat room with designated members with some defined purpose. Ideally, for client portals, you would create a single-channel guest for your client. These users can only access a single channel and cannot see other team members.

Slack takes security and your privacy into consideration, offering strong data encryption in transit and at rest. You can read more about Slack's privacy policy at https://slack.com/privacy-policy and more about their data security measures in their white paper at https://slack.com /security.

Many of Slack's core features are free but come with limitations. For instance, in the free version you can search up to 10,000 messages. There is also a limit on the number of applications you can integrate with Slack. If you go with the Standard plan ($8/user per month), the archive and integration limitations are removed. If you want more support and to be able to export all of your message history for compliance reasons, Slack has a Plus plan ($15/user per month) that offers these benefits.

EXPAND YOUR HORIZON WITH A REMOTE OFFICE

In May 2017, *USA Today* published a study that indicated 62 percent of remote workers fear that other employees do not think they are working as hard as their peers. It is a stigma that needs to dissipate as more companies integrate some amount of remote work into their environment. Remote workers can be slackers, or they can be workaholics, just like in-office workers. The key to changing the way you view this working arrangement lies in trust in your workplace culture. Remote office workers need to be measured on their output and results, not the amount of face time.

There will inevitably be times in your career where you will be outside of the brick-and-mortar office for extended periods of time. Maybe you have children or grandchildren in need of attentive care, or medical concerns preventing you from reaching the office. If you are thinking about expanding to allow remote offices for yourself or colleagues, here are a few tips to guide you:

1. Make sure you and any remote worker on your team have the technology tools you need.
2. Adopt guidelines to convey what is expected from remote workers; this will help ease the fear of misunderstanding between you and your team members.
3. When it comes to getting the right technology, 64 percent of remote workers surveyed in the *USA Today* study said that use of video improved team relationships. Speaking to someone face-to-face, allows you to pick up on body language cues as well as what people are saying.

Remember, the technology tools are available to make remote work seamless; your office may just need to integrate them into your workflow. Keep in mind that understanding how to use the tools is as important as having the tools.

MOVING BEYOND THE REMOTE OFFICE TO A VIRTUAL OFFICE

For some lawyers, especially older lawyers who have started to transition into retirement, a virtual practice offers a way to continue practicing longer. Virtual law practices have become more mainstream, especially as attorneys scale back their practice and look toward retirement. Mobile and web-based technology drives the expansion of virtual practices.

In her guide *Virtual Law Practice: How to Deliver Legal Services Online* (available in the American Bar Association webstore), Stephanie Kimbro defines a virtual law practice as "a professional law practice that exists online through a secure portal and is accessible to both the client and the lawyer anywhere the parties may access the Internet." While an exact definition of a "virtual law practice" remains open for discussion, there are some common characteristics, which you will need to establish should you go in this direction:

1. **Establish a secure client portal**.
   We refer to a secure client portal as

a client-specific, password-protected portal (or *extranet*) where a lawyer and client can interact and transact business online. To access a portal, clients must create a username and password that will allow them to access all the information, including communications, related to their matter that has been input, uploaded, or documented within the secure space.

2. **Set up a web-based area for client interaction**. At the minimum, you should have a website set up. Your website primarily conveys static information about the firm and its lawyers. What more could your website do? You could offer a means for the client to communicate with the firm generally or each individual attorney specifically. You could incorporate calendaring features into your website, allowing clients to access you and feel in control of their scheduling. You could even incorporate the secure client portal

discussed above and provide clients with matter updates.

3. **Enjoy telecommuting from home, or drive to a coffee shop and practice if you want to.**

CLOUD COMPUTING

As mentioned in the Introduction, cloud computing has become an equalizer across hardware and software platforms. Cloud computing is the practice of using a network of remote servers hosted on the Internet to store, manage, and process your data, rather than keeping it on your local server or personal computer. At one time it was thought to be synonymous with cloud storage (your Dropbox and Google Docs accounts), but cloud computing has evolved to incorporate software as a service (SAAS), platform as a service (PAAS), and infrastructure as a service (IAAS). More acronyms keep developing so here is a brief breakdown to make sense of it all:

SAAS. This is usually the more familiar form of cloud service for lawyers. It is basically a software you use, usually entirely on the web. Some software may have a plug-in you need to download to use, but the majority can be used anywhere you can access a web browser. Examples of SAAS you may be familiar with include Dropbox, Google Apps, and Box.

PAAS. This is often the layer under SAAS that drives it, providing the platform on which the cloud-based services can be developed and deployed.

IAAS. This is the fundamental building block of your cloud services. This consists of highly automated and scalable computer resources complemented by cloud storage and network capabilities.

What Is a Plug-In?

A plug-in, also sometimes called an "add-in" or "add-on," is a software component that adds specific features to your existing computer program. It allows you to run special features or functions that the software does not normally run.

IAAS and PAAS are more advanced concepts then you probably need, but SAAS is a pretty common term that you will see thrown around the more you use cloud services. You need not worry too much about it, but just understand that it means your software exists in the cloud. This means you do not have to worry about updating it or solving glitches or bugs. It also means you do not own the software. Depending on how the Terms of Service read (and they will all have their own Terms of Service for you to scour through), you may or may not own the data stored in the cloud service. That is something you need to pay attention to: who owns the data you store. This includes asking questions like:

1. Who has access to the data?
2. Where is it stored (geographically) and are there any privacy issues with the location? For example, some foreign countries may have different rights and remedies.

A little due diligence on the front end can save you time and money in the long run, not to mention the peace of mind you have from knowing your data is secure.

TEAM VIEWER FOR REMOTE ACCESS TO YOUR COMPUTER

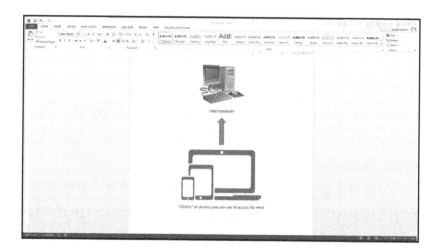

If you need access to your computer beyond the files set up in cloud storage, it might be time to set up remote access software. Remote access software lets you remotely control one computer from another. The remote control is just like it sounds: you can take over the mouse and keyboard of the computer and work on it as though you were sitting in front of it. This can be useful if you are trying to show your child or grandchild how to do something, or maybe if they are trying to show you how to do something.

To remotely access a computer, you need to install access software on the computer to which you would like to connect, which is called the *host* computer. This can be your desktop at home or wherever your main computer resides. Once that is done, then another computer or device with the right *credentials* (the host computer's identifying information and the access software) can connect to the *host* and control it. The computer or device you use to access the *host* is called the *client*.

You do not have to understand all the terminology, or have any IT background, to get started using remote access software. The easiest one we found is TeamViewer. One of the best things about TeamViewer is that it is free for personal use (they have subscription plans for commercial users, but you likely will not need all those features). TeamViewer provides users with highly secure end-to-end encryption.

To start, as we mentioned previously, you need to download the remote access software to the computer you want to access (the *host*). To download TeamViewer, go to their website at https://www.teamviewer .us/. The current iteration of TeamViewer is TeamViewer 13. You will note on the homepage it reads "Completely free for personal use*" with personal use being limited to computers and devices not being used for business or other commercial tasks. Click the green button that reads "Download Now" to add the software to your computer. Follow the prompts to begin installation. At the TeamViewer 13 Setup window, you are asked "How do you want to proceed?" followed by three options:

- Basic Installation
- Installation to access the computer remotely (unattended)
- Run Only (one-time use)

You want to choose either Basic Installation or Installation to access the computer remotely (unattended). Of the two choices, we recommend you choose the second for unattended access. Also, on this screen you will need to indicate if this is for personal or business use; choose personal use to proceed with free access. The installation will continue and prompt you to set up unattended access. Unattended access means you can access the computer with no one being there and logged into it. You can create a unique name for your computer and a password. As you should with every account containing sensitive information, use a strong password.

Once you have TeamViewer set up on your *host* computer, follow the same steps on your *client* computers, laptops, or handheld devices. TeamViewer assigns a unique identification and password to each device on which it is downloaded, and you will use this identification and password to access the computer remotely. Jot down or save your *host* computer identification and password so you can set it up as a connection on your laptop or other *client* device. Once everything is installed on your main computer and the devices you intend to use, then you are all set.

MOBILE TECHNOLOGY

RULES OF MOBILITY: RULE #1— THE MORE YOU CARRY, THE LESS MOBILE YOU BECOME!

We all move around for business and personal reasons. Depending on what we find ourselves doing and where we find ourselves going, we carry different things with us on the road. Here are some basic and universal truths to guide you in your journeys on the road, make things easier for you, and hopefully save your back! While we created these tips originally for road warriors and business-related travel, we think you will find them useful for personal travel as well.

Allen's First Law of Mobility: "Tools make you mobile by helping you work efficiently and effectively on the road, but the more that you carry with you, the less mobile you become." The same is true for whatever you take with you on vacation. The more you take, the more hassle you will have moving around with it. If you plan to just visit one place, you may not have an issue, especially if you drive there.

If you plan to visit several places on your trip and will use a combination of planes, trains, and automobiles to get from one place to the next, it will apply as much to your clothes as to your work gear. The more you take, the greater the amount of difficulty moving it. As we have gotten older and perhaps wiser, we have learned that traveling with less makes a trip easier and more relaxing.

RULES OF MOBILITY: RULE #2— NATURE ABHORS A VACUUM!

Who said you will never use physics after you get out of school? Simply put, we all have a tendency to fill up whatever case we use. If we start with a large suitcase, we pack more than if we start with a smaller one. If we start with a large brief-case, we inevitably take more with us than we need. Start with a medium-sized case and see if you can move to an even smaller one. Choose your gear carefully and pack as little as you can without impairing your ability to accomplish the goals of your trip.

For example, if you do not have to create a lot of documents or use specialized software that requires a computer, you may find that you only need a tablet to handle Internet access and e-mail and can leave the laptop at home. If you do not plan to do a lot of formal dining, you can leave your formal wear (and maybe your semi-formal wear) at home and take only some casual clothes. Look for things that can serve dual or triple purposes to facilitate cutting back on what you take. We have even found it helpful to get special fast-drying clothing for travel, which allows us to take less with us by washing the clothing on the trip.

RULES OF MOBILITY: RULE #3— IF YOU HAVE TO CARRY A LOT OF STUFF, GET SOME WHEELS!

You will likely have occasions when you have to pack a lot of gear to do whatever you set out to do, whether it represents work or play. For example, if you travel out of town for a trial or an arbitration, you will need much more equipment than might be required for a pleasure trip. When you simply have to take a lot of gear with you, use a larger case with wheels and save your back. There is no reason to prove you are still young or strong enough to put it in a duffel bag and toss it over your shoulder like a Continental soldier. Do that long enough and the older you get, the greater the likelihood you will develop joint prob-lems. If you have reached senior status, you have nothing to prove and prove noth-ing by carrying luggage without wheels. We have found that the most convenient and, in our opinion, the best cases have four sets of double wheels. The older style (with two sets of wheels) works fine, but you still have to carry more of the weight of the bag. The four-wheel bags carry vir-tually all of the weight, generally roll more smoothly, and can actually help you bal-ance better when you walk (almost func-tioning as a cane). Also, in a pinch, you will find it far easier to wheel two of the bags with four sets of wheels than schlep two of the bags with two sets of wheels. (Hint: turn the bags so the handles touch each other and roll them together.)

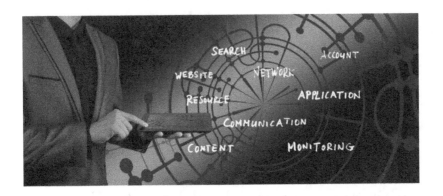

RULES OF MOBILITY: RULE #4— LEVERAGE THE CLOUD TO PROTECT YOUR DATA

No matter where you go these days, you will probably have Internet access available to enable you to move information in and out of the cloud. Take advantage of that. To practice "safe Internet travel," prophylactically encrypt your information (password protecting it with a secure password or phrase) and store it in the cloud before you leave, download it, unencrypt it and use it when you need it, and then re-encrypt it and put it back in the cloud when you finish with it. Why? Because you cannot lose what you do not have with you.

If you carry the information with you on your laptop, iPad, or an external drive, you could misplace the drive, iPad, or laptop or have it stolen. Either way you have put the information at risk and created a possible ethical issue for yourself or, if it is your personal information, put yourself at risk for identity theft. Hopefully, you will have had the foresight to encrypt the confidential information with a secure password before losing it, minimizing your risk. But, if you store properly encrypted information in the cloud and someone steals your laptop or iPad or you misplace your external drive (on which you have also properly encrypted your personal and confidential data you carry), you have not lost the data as you can easily download it from the cloud storage, you have no ethical problem, and you can continue to use the data as required on your other devices (or on the new one you get to replace the one that got lost or stolen).

RULES OF MOBILITY: RULE #5— IF YOUR EQUIPMENT DOES NOT HAVE ITS OWN INTERNET ACCESS, BRING YOUR OWN HOTSPOT

Public Wi-Fi connections expose you to greater risk than secure private connections. You can limit your exposure while maintaining Internet access by carrying your own secure cellular-based hotspot. Most carriers offer these devices as stand-alones. Many smartphones and tablets can also double as hotspots. We prefer the stand-alone devices as they generally work faster and using them avoids draining power from your phone or tablet. If you travel out of the United States, however, you will find that, generally, your domestic Internet service provider (ISP) has grown far more (perhaps prohibitively) expensive. You can avoid that problem by getting one of the international hotspot devices now available. The devices cost little, will allow connection by multiple devices, and they will sell you small buckets of access time for far less than your domestic provider's rates. If you will spend substantial time in a region covered by a single local ISP, you can also buy a SIM card and access to the Internet through the local ISP, at far more reasonable rates. Using a SIM card from an ISP other than your normal provider requires that you have an unlocked device. Some ISPs lock devices to their system until your contract with them expires. Check that out before you go.

The availability of free or low cost Wi-Fi in hotels and coffee shops has grown dramatically in recent years. Many people find the availability of free Wi-Fi too tempting to use their own paid for access. We can understand that sentiment, but, if you use the Wi-Fi in your hotel or the local café or coffee shop, you need to take extra precautions to protect yourself and your data. Get access to and set up a virtual private network (VPN). Think of a VPN as a safe tunnel through cyberspace.

"BACK TO MY MAC" FOR REMOTE ACCESS TO YOUR MAC COMPUTER

Back to My Mac is an iCloud feature that is useful if you are working remotely from your office and need to do something, or to help troubleshoot another person's Mac computer. The feature lets you connect to your Mac over the Internet or by using another Mac. When you connect to your home Mac from a remote Mac you can copy files or do anything you like to those files between both machines. You can also see a live version of the screen on the Mac you are accessing from the Mac you use. You can control the home Mac as if you were there using the computer in person. This extends to running apps on the office/home Mac even if you do not have these installed on the Mac you use to access Back to My Mac.

Back to My Mac is a handy tool for anyone needing files they do not have with them who do not want to use public file sharing services (especially confidential files, financial data, and so on). It is also useful to those who need to access a certain application they do not have installed on the Mac they are using

To use Back to My Mac, you must enable it on your computer. To do this, first open System Preferences, then go into iCloud (in the Internet and Wireless group) and enable Back to My Mac (make sure the box next to it is checked). Next go back to System Preferences and into Sharing. There you will want to make sure that Screen Sharing, File Sharing, and Remote Login are all checked, and that access is set for all users if you want to access it from any Mac.

Once you are set up, to access files using Back to My Mac on a remote Mac, open up Finder and you will see all of the Macs now connected to your iCloud ID. Back to My Mac requires that both Macs be logged into the same Apple ID.

Screen sharing, or seeing and controlling another user's screen, takes a little more finesse.

Screen Sharing is available through Messages on your Mac. To share the screen, both participants must have an Apple ID.

Check that you are logged into yours inside System Preferences. Next go to iCloud and sign in with your Apple ID. The person you wish to screen share with must also log in. You also need to use the e-mail associated with the Apple ID of the person you wish to see. You need to be running OS X Yosemite or newer.

To use Screen Sharing, both parties must launch Messages.

1. Send a new message to the Apple ID of the person you are trying to access.
2. Next, click Details in the top right-hand corner.
3. Click on the screen share icon—you will find this icon beside the telephone and video icon at the top right of the details screen. It will look like two small rectangles.
4. If the person you wish to share the screen with is logged in, you can tap the icon, then choose "Ask to Share Screen" from the drop-down menu that appears.
5. The other person will receive a notification asking if he or she wishes

to share the screen. This needs to be accepted for screen sharing to work. Once the other person permits access, a window will appear on your desktop displaying the other screen.

6. Click on the window and you can use your mouse to move the cursor on the other display and highlight the area of interest inside a white circle; the remainder of the screen will be grey.

If it is not already apparent, both terminals need to be Mac computers for Back to My Mac and screen sharing to work.

RECHARGE ANYWHERE WITH A PORTABLE POWER BANK

If you find yourself out on the move a lot, you may find your devices are running out of power before you are. You can carry your own personal storage of power to recharge your devices wherever you are. When considering external batteries, remember that the higher the capacity, the more charge you get. One of our favorites is the Anker PowerCore+ 20100mAh battery pack ($41.99, Amazon.com). The 20100mAh (milliamp hours) mentioned in the product description represents the battery capacity. The PowerCore+ packs a remarkable amount of charge in a tiny package. With 20,100mAh, it can fully charge one MacBook, one iPhone, and one iPad Air 2 on a single charge. If you are only using it to charge your phone, it can charge a phone seven times with no recharge. When it is time to refuel, you will need to plug it in for about eight hours to get fully recharged.

If you want the benefit of an extra battery, but you do not want the burden of carrying around an additional device, consider getting a battery-extending protective phone case. Check out the Mophie Juice Pack lineup. Mophie offers many battery charging cases for iPhone, Samsung, and HTC phones. The best place to start looking is with the Mophie Juice Pack ($59.95 to $129.95, depending on your phone model, available at Mophie.com). Mophie makes these battery charging phone cases for all the currently supported Apple iPhone models and the Samsung Galaxy, along with a few other models you will find listed on their website. For example, the Juice Pack for the iPhone 7 carries 2,525mAh battery capacity, allowing it to extend the life of your phone battery for up to 27 hours. It measures 5.90 inches $\times$ 2.80 inches $\times$ 0.65 inch and weighs in at 3.51 ounces. The case is designed with a soft-touch plastic that makes it easier to hold. Inside are rubberized support pads to protect your phone from the everyday wear and tear it encounters. With priority charge and sync, your phone will get recharged first when connected, and then the Juice Pack case recharges itself. It comes in many colors for customization (including black, navy, red, gold, and rose gold).

If you carry a small bag around, check out the Anker PowerCore + mini, 3350mAh Portable Charger ($14.99, Amazon.com). This is one of the most popular power banks in Anker's lineup. This tubular portable charger measures 3.7 inches × 0.9 inch × 0.9 inch. It can fit comfortably in your pocket and will take up little real estate in your work bag or purse. The 3,350mAh capacity can give you a full charge on an iPhone 8 or at least 80 percent of Samsung's Galaxy S8 and comparable smartphones.

If you carry more than one electronic device with you, or are a heavy phone user, upgrade the capacity of the power bank you carry with you. We have found some very functional 8,000mAh power banks in slim and easily pocketable cases at Costco for $15 each (but you have to buy a package of two).

For those of you with phones that allow charging by laying the phone on a charging pad, they now have power banks that support this type of charging. The advantage of such devices is that you need not have a cable to charge the phone.

RECHARGE YOUR LAPTOP ANYWHERE WITH SPECIALIZED POWER BANKS

Every time one of the authors (Ashley) gets ready to walk out the door, she runs through a mental checklist that consists of:

✔ Keys
✔ Cell phone
✔ Wallet

Since her remote workload has increased, she has now added a fourth check to the list: to include a power bank capable of recharging laptops. While less common, a few choices are available on Amazon.com. A power bank is a portable battery charger for your digital devices, such as smartphones, tablets, and laptops. It extends the battery life of your devices if you find yourself somewhere without power, like on a long flight, on the beach, or during a hurricane.

Power banks built to charge laptops typically have a higher charge capacity (mAh) than ones built solely for smartphones and tablets. This makes sense because the battery to power a laptop is larger than that of a cell phone or tablet. Newer laptops are running on smaller, lower capacity batteries. Generally, we recommend you look for the largest capacity you are comfortable traveling with (often larger capacity correlates to larger size). However, recently, airlines adopted new regulations limiting the batteries you can check in your baggage and the type you can bring on board in carry-ons. We will cover the details of what batteries are allowed in another tip, but if you plan on using this power bank to extend your laptop's life during airplane travel, check if it is allowed as a carry-on before you bring it with you. Transportation Security Administration (TSA) agents have confiscated noncompliant power banks. If you use a power bank with file storage capability, this can escalate to an even bigger problem if you are storing sensitive data.

Current regulations permit up to 100 watt hours per battery. Some batteries and power banks will tell you the watt hours, but if the one you are interested in does not, you can calculate it yourself. To calculate watt hours, multiply the volts (V) by the ampere hours (Ah).

For example:

> A 12 volt battery (12V) that is rated to eight ampere hours (8 Ah) would ultimately be 96 watt hours (12 × 8 = 96).

Most of the power banks report their capacity in mAh, so you would take that number and divide by 1,000 to get the ampere hours and then go forward with the original formula.

Here are some power banks for your consideration:

Model	Cost	Available at	Review
Crave PowerPack CRVPP101 50,000 mAh	$149.99	Amazon.com	Pro: lots of power in a small package Con: not airline compliant
Dell Power Companion PW7015L	$94.99	TigerDirect .com	Pro: lightweight 18,000mAh battery Con: limited to Dell users
Portable Laptop Battery Pack by ChargeTech– 36,000mAh Capacity	$150.00	Amazon.com	Pro: TSA-approved at 99.8 watt hours Con: designed for MacBook, MacBook Air, and MacBook Pro
Aceyoon Laptop Battery Pack 20,000mAh	$82.98	Amazon.com	Pro: rated 74 watt hours (TSA-approved), multiple adapters to accommodate the most devices in our sampling Con: at 20,000mAh, it is at the lower end with Dell, but still a great choice for airplane travel

FROM MANY, ONE

All of our electronic devices require power. We will need to recharge them at some point on the road. While we can use a power bank in the short term, longer travels will ultimately require that we plug them into an outlet to recharge the devices (and, for that matter, the power banks). While most devices come with a separate charger, you need not use that charger on the device. Most chargers will interchange handily among many devices. That means you need not bring the chargers for all of your devices. If you only brought one charger supplied with your devices, that might actually enable you to charge them all, as the majority have a Universal Serial Bus (USB) port to allow you to plug a cable into the port and the other end into the device to supply the power to recharge its battery.

As you will probably want or need to charge more than one device at a time, bringing a single charger does not provide for efficiently completing the recharging process . . . or does it? If you do not use the charger supplied by the manufacturer of the device, but instead go online (Amazon .com carries several models of these) and look for a single charger that will accommodate multiple USB cables, that charger can take care of all of your needs handily and only using one electrical outlet (electrical outlets often come in short supply). If you go to Amazon.com and search for a "multi USB charger," it will provide you with a selection of several in a variety of configurations. You can get our favorite, the USB C Charger RAVPower 6 Port Type C 60W Wall Charger 5V 3A Fast Charger for $28.95. We like this device as it provides a sufficient number of outlets for us, has adequate power, costs very little, and works well. We also like it as it updated the previous version (which had six USB A outlets) to the current configuration with five USB A outlets and one USB C outlet. The addition of the USB C outlet means that the charger will also work with USB C to USB C cables, such as those that come with Apple's Mac-Book. The device also works well for international travel as it will accept input from 110V–240V supplies, which means that when you leave the United States, you do not need a transformer, only an adapter for the plug receptacle of wherever you visit.

PROTECT THE SCREENS OF YOUR MOBILE DEVICES

Because of the way we use them, mobile devices such as smartphones, tablets, and e-readers have a higher risk of incurring damage than desktop computers, particularly to the display. Mobile devices usually come with displays made of glass or plastic. Despite manufacturers' claims that the materials used for their displays have incredible strength, the fact remains that many displays get damaged. The most common ways to damage devices is by dropping the device and cracking the screen, scratches to the screen, and the occasional hungry Labrador retriever mistaking it for a chew toy. While nothing can guarantee that the display will not shatter or scratch, you can reduce the risk of shattering and greatly reduce the risk of scratching the display by protecting it with a shield.

Surface scratches are even more common than cracks. For example, people do not think twice about dropping their phone into their bag and letting it bounce around with keys, pens, and any number of pointy objects. To help protect from this, the first step to protecting the display is to get a screen protector. When choosing a screen protector, remember the three Fs: fit, finish, and feel. Choose a protector designed for your specific model of device, so it will FIT your screen properly. Not all devices have speakers, cameras, or home buttons in the same place. You do not want the protector to inhibit your access to any of the device's features. The screen protector should also FEEL as good as the screen underneath. Years ago, most screen protectors were plastic, but now the trend is tempered glass since it installs better and easier and appears to provide better protection. It does not peel around the edges like plastic did. You may not find tempered glass protectors for all mobile devices yet, but you can find them for many, if not most, smartphones. We have moved to tempered glass screen protectors for all of our smartphones and tablets. Whether you prefer a matte or gloss finish is a personal choice. Also note that some manufacturers offer screen protectors that provide additional functionality, such as privacy enhancement and glare reduction. If you use your mobile devices where others can see the screens (such as on an airplane or in a crowded air terminal), a privacy screen gives you enhanced security against information theft.

Here is a table of some nice protectors you might consider. We noted the model referenced in the cost estimate, but they may have other models to suit your needs.

Model	Cost	Available at	Why we like it
IQ Shield	$8.95 (3-pk, iPhone X)	Amazon .com	Scratch-resistant tempered glass
Auideas 3D 9H Curved Protector	$9.99 (Galaxy S9)	Amazon .com	99.99% high-definition transparent, curved to fit the Galaxy S9 Plus
Geelie Privacy Screen Protector	$6.99 (Galaxy Note 8)	Amazon .com	Full screen coverage, privacy protection when viewed at less than a 45° angle
ZAGG InvisibleShield	$23.49 (iPhone 6–8)	Amazon .com	ZAGG has a strong reputation, high quality, and a nice warranty tied to their product

The second step to protecting a display is to get a case for the device with a cover that flips over the display. You have lots of choices for both display protectors and cases with display covers. Check places like Best Buy, Amazon.com, Fry's, and the online stores for your device (i.e., the Apple Store for iPhones). Service providers (like Sprint, AT&T, T-Mobile, and so on) also generally carry a selection of such devices. Some of the covers double as wallets or stands or both, making them multifunctional and very handy. If you prefer a case without a cover, look for one that has a ridge that sits a bit higher than the display. That will afford some protection if you drop the device face down. Most of the cases that provide covers to go over the display afford less overall protection and more scratch protection and conversely. Many of the cases that do not provide covers provide better shock protection but at the cost of greater bulk.

GET HELP NAVIGATING THE OPEN ROAD

Distracted driving is a major issue for many drivers. Whether it is your phone buzzing with notifications for new text messages, the Global Positioning System (GPS) reminding you for the third or fourth time about a turn you missed two blocks ago, or kids fiddling with the radio station, it is everywhere in the car. According to the National Conference of State Legislatures, as of 2017, 47 states plus the District of Columbia, Puerto Rico, Guam, and the U.S. Virgin Islands have all banned text messaging for all drivers; Missouri prohibits text messaging by teenage drivers. Add to that, 14 states and the District of Columbia, Puerto Rico, Guam, and the U.S. Virgin Islands prohibit any use of a handheld cell phone while driving (including for calls and GPS). Thirty-eight states have banned all cell phone use (even hands-free usage) by teenage drivers. All this legislation makes it worth adding hands-free technology to your mobile tool kit.

More and more carmakers are integrating head-up displays (HUDs) into their vehicles. A HUD is a digital transparent image projected onto the windshield of a car, displaying the same information you would get from the dashboard. By displaying this data in the same place where a driver should be keeping his or her eyes (out the window ahead of the driver), HUDs can reduce the time that your attention is spent looking around the car for phones or checking the radio. More time with your eyes on the road means fewer accidents, and an all-around safer driving experience. It is worth noting that it only works on cars made after 1996. You will find this technology in the BMW 7 Series, Volvo XC90, Chevrolet Corvette Stingray, Mazda3, Lexus RX, and Jaguar XF, to name a few. If you are in the market for a new car and have the option to go for a factory-installed HUD, go with it. Generally, the add-on will run you around a few hundred dollars extra and is almost certainly worth the cost.

If you are interested in the technology, but not ready to take the plunge, test the waters with some of the apps on the market that project onto your display from your iPhone or Android device. Lately there have been a few apps (Sygic GPS Navigation & Maps, Hudway Go, Speedometer 55 GPS Speed & HUD, and so on) popping up both in the iTunes and Google Play app stores that provide a lot of the same functionality you would expect from an integrated HUD display, except with none of the hassle of installation or getting all the wiring right between incompatible cars. The apps work by brightly displaying a reverse image of your speed (tracked through the phone's internal GPS) on the windshield when the phone is mounted on top of the dashboard itself. Your windshield then reflects this image back to you with any information the app collects.

TECHNOLOGY FOR YOUR HOME

SET UP A WI-FI NETWORK IN YOUR HOME

Setting up a network in your home involves pretty much the same process as setting it up in your office, but you will have a few additional considerations. While we will reiterate some of the basics here, we refer you to the Wi-Fi tips in the Office Technology chapter of this book for most of the information about setting up a Wi-Fi network and focus on the different considerations. The first step remains the acquisition of broadband Internet access through a provider. You will also need to obtain a Wi-Fi router with the ability to set wired and wireless (or just wireless) networks. You can easily find Wi-Fi routers through Amazon.com, or at Best Buy, Fry's, Costco, or just about anywhere else that they sell modern electronic equipment. Often providers, such as Xfinity, will have equipment they can provide. Note, however, that the equipment they have ranges from merely adequate to quite good and you want to end up with the higher end of their equipment.

If you do not already have connectivity with the Internet service provider (ISP) that you plan to use, give some serious thought to the location of the primary connection to the provider's equipment. That will be the spot where, most likely, you will put your principal equipment (modem/router) for connectivity. It is possible to put it in another location, but that will probably require that someone run a hardwired connection to that point. You want a clear signal to go throughout your building to everywhere you will want or need connectivity. You greatly increase the likelihood of accomplishing that if you keep your equipment away from potentially conflicting signals (i.e., other routers or electrical equipment) and away from substantial walls and/or furniture that might block or impair the signal's ability to move through the building. It is not unusual to have many signal-generating sources in your house. Places to avoid include the kitchen and within several feet of television sets or other routers. If you have Xfinity as a cable provider and as an Internet provider and also have their burglar/smoke alarm system, you will have at least two routers from Xfinity (they put the alarm system on a separate router when they set it up). There is nothing wrong with multiple routers per se, but you need to know that they can interfere with each other; sometimes the technicians either do not know or forget about that. Remind them to keep the routers a few feet away from each other to minimize signal interference.

If you will want connectivity on more than one floor, you will do best with your router on the highest floor in your house. Signals travel down better than they travel up.

Connect the router to your broadband network and follow the directions provided with the router to access the router and set up the network. Give the network a name (preferably not your name, your office's name, or your address) and passwords. Most routers will want two passwords, one for administrative access and the other for general use. Use strong passwords for both to protect access and the confidentiality of your data. (See "Set Up a Wi-Fi Network in Your Office" in the

Office Technology chapter for an explanation of a strong password.)

Keep both passwords secure. You, your spouse (or functional equivalent), and maybe a trusted friend or adult child should be the only ones with access to the passwords.

If you will do legal work at home, set up at least two networks in your house, one for office work and the other for you and the family for personal use. YES, we really do recommend that you change the network when you move from office to personal matters. Switching from one network to another will prove most easy to accomplish and gives you some protection for confidential data. Also, importantly, do not leave your computer containing confidential client data at home and connected to the personal network, as you risk compromising confidentiality. Either keep the office data securely in the cloud or safely stored on an external hard disk you disconnect from the network and the computer when you do not need to access the data. (See the section "Set Up a Guest Wi-Fi Network in Your Office" in the Office

Technology chapter of this book for further information about the process of setting up a secondary network.)

If you have guests you will allow to access the Internet on your network, consider setting up a third network for guest use. (See the section "Set Up a Guest Wi-Fi Network in Your Office" in the Office Technology chapter of this book for further information about setting up a tertiary network; the process for the third, fourth, and additional networks is the same as for the second.)

In the best of all worlds, you will end up with a strong wireless signal throughout your house and into your yard, enabling you to use your electronic devices anywhere around your property and to take advantages of the ability to access the Internet, stream music or video, and handle your e-mail anywhere in your house.

Just to put things in perspective, one of the authors has six wireless networks in his house: a 2.4 gigahertz (GHz) and a 5.0 GHz network for business use and the same for personal use, a 2.4 GHz network for the alarm system, and a 2.4 GHz network for guests to use. The 2.4 and 5.0 networks were chosen as the 2.4 works a bit slower but provides better coverage throughout the house and the 5.0 offers better speed. Why does he have this many networks? Because he can! Seriously, though, good reason exists for doing that, as while you can get by with fewer networks, having the options does sometimes come in handy, particularly when you want to reach the Internet and discover a new dead spot in the 5 GHz network.

If, after setting up your network, you experience difficulties with its operation, see the section "Troubleshooting Your Wi-Fi Network" in the Office Technology chapter of this book.

SET UP A WIRELESS NETWORK WITH THE ORBI WI-FI SYSTEM

A wireless router takes the Internet data from your modem and projects it out either wirelessly or via cable. The modem is connected to your cable company's coaxial cable or the telephone company's digital subscriber line (DSL) phone line, depending on which service you use.

The Netgear Orbi Whole Home Mesh WiFi System ($199.99, Amazon.com) is a wide-range wireless mesh router for your home or office. If you have a large home or office space and find yourself with dead zones depending on where you are at, this system is worth looking into. The same situation can occur if you have an unusual layout (i.e., over two stories, interior brick walls); if so, you may have encountered these problems too. The availability of Wi-Fi-enabled smart devices continues to increase in homes and offices, creating a need to improve the reach of your wireless network. Having a Wi-Fi security camera connected to your doorbell does little good if it is too far out of your wireless range to connect to the network. The Orbi has a high price tag, but it delivers high-speed Internet in a wide range. If you have a lot of smart home technology, it is worth investing in your home network.

The Orbi's strong signal comes from its tri-band network and the six high-performance antennae that surround the device, encased by the tower. This allows the Orbi to out-perform competitors. Tests run by Tom's Guide indicated that at five feet from the hub, the Orbi was 19 percent faster than Google Wifi, 34 percent faster than the

Linksys Velop, and 50 percent faster than the Ubiquiti AmpliFi HD.

Out of the box, the Orbi comes across bulkier than other wireless routers. The main system is a white tower-shaped device that measures 8.9 inches tall. You can use it as a bookend on your shelf, but it is difficult to hide. The top is lined with light-emitting diode (LED) lights that are color-coded to indicate the status of your wireless network. At start-up, the device will glow white around the top. When everything functions properly, it will have a soft blue glow. If it glows amber, then your Internet connection is weak; if it is magenta, then your connection is gone.

Setup is simple. If you purchase an Orbi and satellite combo (for coverage up to 3,500 feet), the devices come already paired together. Installation does not require you to know anything about Ethernet, Internet protocol (IP) addresses, or encryption. You do not have to install an app (although one is available for Android and iOS). Once everything is powered on, go to https://www .netgear.com/home/products/networking/ orbi/orbilogin.aspx in your web browser.

There the Orbi software will do a network check and the router will be set up.

Reviews have mentioned problems setting up the Orbi with the latest Mac operating systems. The belief was that the software contained a bug. We suspect that the problem has been solved, as we set up an Orbi network in a two-story house running primarily Mac devices, all with the most current operating systems at the time (iOS 11 and OS X High Sierra). We have not had any problems with the devices and converting to iOS 12 and OS X Mojave has not had any impact on the functionality of the Orbi devices. Whatever the problem was (if there was a problem with the Orbi) has apparently been resolved (at least as far as we can tell).

HIRE A VIRTUAL ASSISTANT AT HOME: AMAZON'S ALEXA (ECHO AND DOT)

Smart home technology providers are generating more and more consumer-friendly products every year, making it easy to get started building your smart home. "Smart home" is the term used to define a residence with appliances and features that can communicate with one another and can be controlled remotely. For instance, you can check who is ringing your doorbell, reset the thermostat, turn off water sprinklers, or any number of mundane tasks without ever setting foot in your home. You do not even have to be in the same country. Maybe not even the same planet, but NASA has not let us test that theory yet. The technology generally offers users convenience, along with saving time, money, and energy.

One of the easiest "smart" home gadgets to set up is the Amazon Echo ($99.99, Amazon .com). Amazon launched its Echo series of smart speakers in 2015. Since then, it has expanded from the Echo (a tower-shaped speaker) to the Echo Dot (a hockey-puck shaped speaker, $49.99, Amazon.com), and 2017 brought us the Echo Show (a larger speaker with video screen for video/voice calling, streaming, and so on, $229.99, Amazon.com). All the devices connect to the voice-controlled digital assistant service, Alexa, which responds to the name. Alternative words you can use to "wake" or activate the devices include "Amazon," "Echo," or "Computer." The devices are capable of:

- Voice interaction
- Voice conferencing
- Video conferencing (if you have the Echo Show or Spot)
- Music playback
- Making to-do lists
- Setting alarms
- Streaming podcasts
- Playing audiobooks
- Providing weather and traffic reports
- Controlling smart home technology
- Providing sports schedules and scores
- Providing general research information
- Answering trivia questions

Setting up the Amazon Echo is simple. You start by plugging in the speaker, then go to your smartphone and download and open the Amazon Alexa app. The app will go through a series of prompts to help you complete the setup. The Echo is a Bluetooth speaker (meaning it uses Bluetooth technology to connect to your devices); however, it connects to your wireless Internet to process voice commands. You will need an Amazon.com account to use the Echo and Alexa (we highly recommend you get one anyway if you do not already have one; it is a great place for online shopping).

There are many ways Amazon Echo can help around the house, including:

1. **Medication reminders**. You can set up reminders to take medications at a specific time. Just say, "Alexa, remind me to take my medicine at 8:00 a.m. every day." You can set as many reminders as necessary to cover multiple medications or different times of day. You can also be more specific if you want Alexa to remind you to take certain medications at certain times.

2. **She will not judge you for asking what day or time it is, no matter how often you ask**. Anyone who struggles with memory can ask, "Alexa, what day is it?" or, "Alexa, what time is it?" Alexa will always be happy to give the answers.

3. **Alexa can entertain you with music, audiobooks, or radio**. You can tell Alexa to play an audiobook, or read an e-book from your Amazon Kindle account, or find music that suits your mood. If you have little ones running around, you can try, "Alexa, tell me a children's story."

4. **Alexa is always good for a laugh**. Grandkids especially like this one. Just say, "Alexa, tell me a joke." You can even make it seasonally appropriate by saying "Alexa, tell me a Halloween joke."

5. **Alexa the lifeline**. If you have a problem remembering a piece of information from some time ago or just want to know current information about something, Alexa can help. Notwithstanding that she has the entire Internet to draw from,

Alexa has no answers for some seemingly basic, but important questions. For example, you can always get the weather or the time for any major city in the world and most minor ones, and discover the schedule of a sports team or the current score in an ongoing game. You can even find out who Trump just fired. However, when faced with truly important questions, such as "why are Trix for kids?" or "what's the difference between a left Twix and a right Twix?" Alexa came up short. She had no idea.

6. **Alexa the babysitter**. For the very young, it will entertain them with music (you choose the genre). For those who have learned to talk, the endless questions they like to ask can get directed to Alexa, who will patiently answer almost all of the questions, no matter how often the child asks the question. Sometimes Alexa will decline to answer a question for one of several reasons, but the most frequent is that Alexa does

not know and cannot find the correct response on the Internet. We have seen children in the five- to seven-year age range spend well over an hour interrogating Alexa and having a wonderful time.

Incidentally, we have inadvertently discovered that if you want to upset Alexa, just call her Siri. We learned that mistake the hard way. We looked at an Echo and said, "Hey, Siri," and Alexa refused to speak to us.

THE ECHO SHOW

We bet you thought this was a theater recommendation. Well, not really; it relates to a new piece of technology from Amazon. Digital Internet-connected personal assistants like Siri, Alexa, and Hey Google have become very popular and have many functions, some of which can actually prove useful. The developers of these personal assistants have provided you with many ways to access them and make use of them. Amazon has created our favorite hardware for this purpose and called it the Echo "Show." You can have the Show in any color you want, as long as you want black or white. You must connect it to your broadband wireless Internet to use it, as it depends on that connection for the information it provides to you.

The Echo Show offers better speakers than the Echo and a large touchscreen display that you can use for video calling any other Echo Show or Amazon Alexa app users. The display can also show you videos from Amazon Prime, display pictures like a digital photo frame, show you weather reports, or provide the lyrics to a song as it streams music. More "skills" are being added by third-party apps. For anyone wanting a gift that lets them communicate with elderly parents, this is a great option to consider. Alexa (the digital assistant that powers the Echo devices) now offers a "drop in" feature, which, if enabled, allows specific authorized contacts to see in to your camera feed regardless of whether you pick up the call. When the user does so, he or she will see a blurred feed for the first ten seconds, during which time the owner can disable the camera or reject the call outright. A notification is displayed on the screen whenever someone is actively viewing your feed. A motion sensor in the Echo Show will notify authorized contacts when it senses you nearby. This may sound a tad creepy, but it also makes sense for keeping an eye on an aging relative.

The Show functions at many levels. It works as an entertainment device, playing both audio and video media, it can order merchandise for you from Amazon.com, and provide a wide variety of factual information that it gathers from the Internet at a very fast speed. It also functions nicely as a communications device (this is one of our favorite uses). Show has a feature called "drop in." You have to set it up in advance with others who also have the Show device, as they have to grant you permission to drop in on them. Once it is set up, you can continue to use it without going through the setup process again for that person. We like the Show as it provides a video and an audio connection to the other person, using the camera on his or her Show to show the person to you, while your camera shows you to him or her. Once set up, you just say, "Alexa, drop in on (insert name of the dropee)." Alexa uses Wi-Fi to connect to the other's Show and the video chat is automatically set up for your use. If you get more than one of these devices, you can also use this feature to have them function as an intercom system, as they will allow you to contact just one or make an announcement to all of them.

Setting up the Show takes a few minutes and very little effort, as does setting up the drop in feature. Drop in makes a wonderful gift and a useful tool for you. It makes it easy to talk to children, grandchildren, other family, and friends in video conference mode. It also offers a way to check up on your pets, if you have such an inclination. Depending on the quality of your broadband connection, the images can be quite good, and with a good Internet connection, you see very little lag between video and audio.

Remember that whenever you approve someone dropping in on you, they can drop in at any time. Also remember that the video comes from the camera in your Show. Accordingly, you might want to think about whether you even want one in your bedroom and, if so, what direction you want to point it.

We have also found another hidden feature of the Show. Young children get a kick out of it. We have seen them stand in front of it and ask it questions for prolonged time periods. That works with any Alexa device, but the Show can also provide images, which helps keep the kids interested.

Since we wrote this tip, Amazon announced an upgraded Show (generation II) that provides a better speaker and a larger screen for the same price ($229). Our units have not yet arrived, so we have not tested them yet. We expect them in short order, as they are supposed to be out by the time this book is published. We have seen the first-generation Shows discounted to $129 in anticipation of the release of the second generation.

SMART HOME TECHNOLOGY— LITEdge SMART PLUG

Continuing our journey into smart home technology, you can control lights or any outlet-powered electronics from an app anywhere with the LITEdge Smart Plug ($12.99/single outlet, Amazon.com) made by Torchstar. You are probably thinking, how can something as mundane as wall power outlets help me? It is the little tweaks you can make around you that add up to a great savings of time and effort. So, what exactly is a "smart" outlet and how can it help you? A smart outlet is a device that plugs into any ordinary electrical outlet. It is also sometimes called a "smart plug" or a "smart switch," and it basically acts like a stoplight for electricity traveling from your outlet to your device.

For example, it would be handy if you travel a lot. You could use this plug and a lamp to turn a light on or off in your front window during the day to look like someone is home even when you are vacationing in the Caribbean. All you would need to do is plug the lamp into one of these outlets, plug the outlet into your power outlet, power the lamp on, and then control whether the power is on or off for the smart outlet through the LITEdge app. The LITEdge app is available in the iOS App Store (for iOS 8 or later) or on Google Play (Android 4.1 or later). Once you download the app, open it on your phone and it will guide you through connecting the plug to your home network. There is no limit on the number of devices you can control, no separate hub required, and no subscription service fees. When you want the lamp off, switch it off in the app and the smart plug will cut the power to it.

You can also use a smart plug to make sure dinner is ready when you get home. While it will not do the prep work for you, you can put everything you need in a slow cooker, turn it on with the settings, then use the smart plug to cut off the power to the outlet until you are ready for it to start. This is an easy way to have dinner ready for the table when you pull up in the driveway.

You could use it to connect to an electric blanket and turn it on 15 minutes before you go to bed to have it toasty and warm for you when you lie down.

The plugs can automate lights if you decorate with those around the holidays.

You can mount a portable fan and use the smart plug to turn it on and off to stay cool in the summertime.

Some users connect their garage door opener to a smart plug to control the garage door. This way if they are out of town for a few days, the garage door is locked.

Using the plugs might not work if the device requires you to push a button to turn it on; however, they can still be useful if you are worried about whether you turned something off. If you have a space heater for example or if you cannot remember whether you turned off the coffee pot or curling iron. With the plug you can cut the power to the outlet from your phone no matter where you are.

Bonus tip: The LITEdge will work with Google Home and the Amazon Echo, if you want to add voice control to the outlet.

SMART HOME TECHNOLOGY— NEST THERMOSTAT

Smartphones have become powerful tools that make life easier, and smart home technology is heading down the same path. Once you have gotten comfortable with smartphone technology, integrating technology systems into your home is the next trend with which to experiment. Transitioning to a smarter home can save you time and money, and improve your home's security, safety, and accessibility. Do not overload your home with gadgets to start enjoying the benefits of an integrated smart home. You can add features piece by piece and design a system around your needs. One easy feature to start with is a smart thermostat, like the Nest thermostat ($249, Nest.com). Nest is on its third generation of this smart, "learning" thermostat, and it has made some nice improvements.

The Nest is simple to install; it will come with everything you need in the box, including a screwdriver, mounting screws, and a mounting base. Nest added a larger, higher-resolution screen and a far-field sensor that can recognize movement from across the room and then display on the screen either the time, temperature, or weather forecast. It continues to excel at learning your schedule and your heating and cooling preferences. Once the Nest learns this, it will then generate a customized energy-efficient schedule based on your preferences. You will want to take a week or so to teach the thermostat your preferences by adjusting the temperature to your comfort level when you come home, setting it somewhere else when you leave, and so on. After about a week you can turn on the auto-schedule and the Nest will use your previous heating/cooling commands along with data from its own sensors and algorithms to create an energy-saving schedule that you can adjust or turn off altogether if you do not like it.

If you are concerned about security with all these connected smart gadgets (and you should always be mindful of security), rest a little easier knowing that the Nest now has two-factor authentication that you can enable. We have gone into two-factor authentication in detail in other books, but, briefly, it is a two-step sign on process. Whereas most authentication is done by entering a username and password, two-factor authentication adds an additional check, usually in the form of a code sent to your phone or e-mail that you can enter to verify that you are you, an actual person, and the one who has the right to access that device.

One drawback to the Nest is a lack of remote sensors that allow you to monitor and control the temperature in individual rooms, as opposed to the entire home. Unless living in a multi-level structure or larger home, most users do not miss this feature. If you live in a large or complex house, check out the Ecobee3.

Bonus tip: If you are nervous about installing a thermostat yourself, you might order the Nest from Amazon.com and add "Expert Installation" to your order. Amazon Services contracts with area service providers to install the devices once you receive the order. This is a nice way to make home improvement almost hassle free.

NIXPLAY DIGITAL PHOTO FRAME

Digital photo frames are a lovely way to display tons of photos at your home or office without purchasing and mounting lots of frames. Changing out photos is substantially easier too, just switch out the memory card or Universal Serial Bus (USB) thumb drive and have all your photos in a slideshow. There are several digital frames from which you can choose. You can even use tablet devices as a digital photo frame, which is a handy trick if you want to have a digital photo frame running at gatherings with family or friends. Here we will offer some guidance on what to look for when buying a digital photo frame, along with a few examples of frames we like that you might want to check out.

For starters, you want your pictures to look as crisp and clear as though they were hanging on the wall in print or canvas. To ensure this clarity, keep the screen resolution of the photo frame in mind. "Screen resolution" refers to the clarity of the text and images displayed on your screen. Higher resolution will produce sharper, clearer images. The resolution is usually indicated as *#### × ####* (e.g., 1,600 × 1,200; 1,024 × 768). This indicates the number of horizontal and vertical pixels on a display screen. Higher resolutions tend to come with a higher price tag, but we want you to understand what you are getting and the tradeoff.

Technology Terms Explained

SCREEN RESOLUTION

Screen resolution refers to the clarity of the text and images displayed on your screen. A higher resolution (indicated by a larger number of pixels) will produce sharper images.

PIXEL

A pixel is a minute area of illumination on a display screen. Many individual pixels compose the images you see on a screen.

ASPECT RATIO

This describes the dimensions of an image by comparing the width to the height and expressing it in ratio form.

Next, consider the screen size of the frame. Frames can range in size from around seven inches up to 20+ inches. Choose a size that will fit comfortably where you want to display it. Just like with resolution, the larger the screen size, the more you will pay.

The trickier concept to remember when choosing a frame is the aspect ratio. Most frames will support a 4:3, 16:9, or 15:9 aspect ratio. Most of your point-and-shoot digital cameras will capture the image with a 4:3 aspect ratio. If the images you want to display have this ratio, then a 4:3 aspect ratio will work best. Displaying images with a 4:3 aspect ratio in a digital photo frame with a 16:9 ratio will result in your images being cropped at the top and bottom to make the image fit. A benefit of the 16:9 aspect ratio is that it gives the images a widescreen feel.

Next, look at the aesthetics of the frame itself. Some displays have a sleek modern look, while others may be encased in a wood frame or metal frame to appear more traditional. Consider whether you want the display to be in portrait or landscape mode and whether you have the option to switch between the two.

Beyond these considerations, you will find many bells and whistles like Wi-Fi-enabled web browsers, streaming Internet radio, text news feeds, and so on. These features may be fun but can also be a little overwhelming. If all you want is to view photos, save the time and a little money and get a basic frame with a USB port.

Now that you know what it is you are looking for, here are a few suggestions you might like:

Nixplay Seed Ten-Inch Wi-Fi Cloud Frame ($169.99, Shop.Nixplay.com). The Nixplay Seed packs a lot of viewing power into a sleek package. There are models available from seven inches up to 13 inches, with customizable frames to suit your personal style. The ten-inch display comes with a 1,024 × 768 high-definition screen that does a great job displaying images. There is a mobile app for your smartphone that can capture the images while you are experiencing the moments and upload them directly to your frame over Wi-Fi. With the Nixplay web app, you can upload photos from your computer or tablet, and access your photos on social media sites like Facebook, Dropbox, Instagram, Picasa, and Flickr. Nixplay also includes a motion sensor feature that turns the frame on when you walk into the room and shuts it off when you leave.

NIX Lux 13-Inch Non-Wi-Fi Frame in Wood ($179.99, Shop.Nixplay.com). The NIX Lux also comes from Nixplay and is offered without the Wi-Fi features but with a nice grain wood design that looks great in the office. This frame is a great alternative if you do not care for the Wi-Fi/ social media integration features of the Seed Cloud frame. It comes with a stunning 1,920 × 1,280 screen resolution with 16:9 aspect ratio. Like the Seed, this frame comes with a motion sensor to turn the display off when no one is in the room.

Pix-Star 10.4-Inch Wi-Fi Cloud Digital Photo ($159.99, Amazon.com). The Pix-Star Cloud frame is available in both 10.4-inch and 15-inch sizes and has the 4:3 aspect ratio good for point-and-shoot digital cameras. You can add photos to this frame through USB, secure digital (SD) cards, or e-mail over the Wi-Fi. The frame comes with its own e-mail address, so you can send photos from any device with e-mail. You can even e-mail images from the frame to anyone's e-mail address.

EMBRACE A DECLUTTERING MANTRA

Some people feel a sense of guilt, fear, or sentimentality when they purge stuff from their office. It is okay and normal to feel those emotional pangs, but letting them stop you from getting rid of stuff and simplifying your life is not okay. For instance, many people feel a sense of guilt when giving away or disposing of something that was given to them. Yielding to this sense will make it difficult to declutter your office space.

Here are some common reasons why people hold onto outdated, arguably useless technology, along with even better reasons to ignore that urge to keep everything:

1. **You cannot bear to part with the item because it holds too much sentimental value**. This holds many people back, especially when it comes to captured memories in photos. One way to clean up and save space here is to invest in a quality digital photo frame. You can use the frames to display all the photos you had cluttering your mantles, end tables, and wall space. If you feel attached to a large accumulation of prized possessions, consider taking photos of them to include in your digital frame. That way you can preserve your favorite memorabilia in a single frame on your desk rather than all over your work space.

2. **You feel guilty getting rid of a present**. One thing to remember here is that gifts are symbols of the love and appreciation between friends and family. Donating or regifting the item is a way to let that love flow wherever the item travels.

3. **You will eventually make something out of all these things**. Maybe

you enjoy scrapbooking in your free time and have amassed a room full of photos and supplies. Maybe you like tinkering in the garage. To simplify your "collection," come up with a specific project and only keep the items you need for that project. The rest you can either let go of or store in a designated facility. Store them in an organized manner if possible, maybe grouped by project, to make it easier to pick up on a project later.

4. **Maybe this is valuable**? Today there is an easy way to determine if something is valuable: Google it. Old magazine issues and childhood toys are rarely valuable unless kept in pristine condition. Some auction houses will provide appraisals for free in hopes of you selling your stuff there, so that may be a good way to answer the question of value and to reduce the clutter simultaneously.

Technology Terms Explained

"Google It"

You may have heard this phrase thrown around a lot since 2000 or so, and you may be wondering what it means. Google is the name of a very popular search engine and "google it" has become a verb phrase to mean look up the answer to your question online in a search engine (Google would prefer you use theirs, but you can use any search engine you want).

To search online, you do not have to type your question as a complete sentence. Instead, pick out the key search terms that describe what it is you are trying to find out. In this context, maybe try searching for "auction houses near me" or "auction house free appraisal Houston."

Getting comfortable with decluttering is a challenge for some, but hopefully understanding these challenges will help you.

GOOGLE HOME

The Google Home Mini is a smart speaker equipped with a Google-powered digital assistant. If one of your goals is to simplify and automate your life, consider picking one up for yourself. For one of the authors (Ashley), one of the means to that end has been adding the Google Home Mini to her office hardware tools. Google's lineup of digital assistants include the Google Home, Google Home Mini, and the Google Home Max. As the names might suggest, Google appears to appeal to users who appreciate minimalism and seek simplification.

The setup for the Mini is fast. You start by downloading the free Google Home app (available for Android or iOS). From there, the app will walk you through the steps. You can connect your Google accounts through the app so the Mini can access your existing information.

Out of the box, the Mini looks like a smooth stone you might see at a spa or during a hot stone massage. It is more visually appealing than its competitor, the Amazon Echo Dot. It is slightly cheaper than the Echo Dot as well. But costs and looks aside, how does it perform for office tasks?

If you incorporate methods like the Pomodoro Technique into your work routine, you could start your interval by saying "Hey Google, set a timer for 25 minutes," to which Google Assistant would respond, "Alright, 25 minutes, starting now." If you have to step out of the office and do not want your timer going off steadily in your absence, you can say, "Hey Google, cancel the timer." Ashley uses this to try to incorporate physical activity into her work day, setting a timer for 55 minutes with the idea to get up and walk around for five minutes to get more steps in the day.

If you use Google apps for e-mail and calendar, you can connect those to the Google Home app. Then when someone sends you a text you can say, "Hey Google, add lunch with Jack at 1:00 p.m. today to my calendar," and within moments the appointment will appear blocked off on your calendar. Unfortunately, it appears that you cannot add to the calendar in the past. For example, when asked to "add conference call with client at 9:30 a.m. to my calendar today," because it was already in the afternoon, Google Assistant tried to add it to the calendar for 9:30 a.m. the next day. When told to edit the entry to today, it failed to add anything.

You can run basic searches simply by posing the question "Hey Google . . ." then follow it with your inquiry:

How many liters are in two gallons?

How much sugar is in a cheesecake?

What does *stare decisis* mean?

When is St. Patrick's Day?

How do you make a Tom Collins?

We could go on, but you get the idea. The Assistant can provide useful reminders at your beck and call, too. Rather than interrupt your workflow, you can say, "OK Google . . . remind me to leave the office at 4:00 today." Or, "Hey Google . . . remind me to call Alexander Bell back in 30 minutes." This can be useful for recurring reminders, such as "Hey Google . . . remind me to take medications at 10:30 a.m. every day."

The more smart technology you have around the office, the more you can do with the Google Home as well. If your office uses one of the supported smart thermostats, you can adjust the temperature around your office. You can have a little fun with it too: you can program phrases to trigger certain actions. For instance, if you set up smart bulbs, you can program the Home Mini to turn off all the lights when you say, "OK Google, Elvis has left the building."

NONDA ZUS SMART CAR CHARGER

This little device performs a lot of functions while plugging into the direct current (DC)-connector of your car. Most car chargers like this are designed for one purpose: to power your smartphone from the 12 volt DC outlet (often called the cigarette lighter) in your car. The Nonda ZUS Smart Car Charger ($34.99, Nonda.co) does more. With a $30+ price tag, it would need to bring a lot to the table, and the ZUS rises to the occasion. For starters, it offers dual USB ports capable of charging two smartphones twice as fast as average car chargers. The exterior of the charger is sleek, smooth, black plastic. The USB ports are backlit, giving the device an overall look of luxury. The backlit feature is also useful when plugging in devices in the dark. Besides this, the ZUS comes with a companion iOS/Android app that provides a host of benefits for users. Once you connect the device to the app and to your car, you can:

- Monitor your car battery health so you can avoid the inconvenience of a drained battery. Identify potential issues by tracking voltage over time and get alerts whenever a battery check is recommended.

- Automatically save your parking location and get help to find your car. Simply open the app and use arrows on a map or the compass dial to find your way back.
- Log your mileage, trip duration, and savings potential for each drive. Swipe to classify business drives for tax deductions and easily export Internal Revenue Service-compliant reports.
- Share your parking location with others via Family Share.
- Receive alerts ten minutes before your parking meter time runs out, allowing you to avoid parking tickets.

The ZUS is a lightweight device, weighing in at less than an ounce. It is constructed with military-grade plastic designed to withstand high temperatures. The Car Battery Health Monitor displays activity for the past seven, 30, or 90 days, and will notify drivers when battery performance falls below optimal levels. The saved parking location is a nice feature, but it is buggy in parking garages. ZUS addresses this by prompting you to enter your location when the car shuts off.

All of this more than justifies the price. One drawback though is that the ZUS mileage logging feature requires a subscription plan. The plan can be an additional $34.99/month or $49.99/year. Going with the yearly subscription is a no-brainer if you intend to use this feature.

CLEAN UP YOUR TECH!

Given how frequently we normally use our devices, it should come as no surprise that the number of germs and grime on the surface can be staggering (worse than the toilet handles in a public restroom). This is especially true of your mobile phone, which has the bad habit of calling your attention to it no matter where your hands have just been. Here are a few simple suggestions for keeping your mobile phone clean, using items you likely already have lying around the house. Before you begin cleaning it, unplug the device and seal off any open ports, if possible.

1. **Use a lint-free or microfiber cloth**. You may have this type of cleaning cloth in your home already if you have eyeglasses, or one may have even come with your phone when you purchased it. This cloth will allow you to remove oily fingerprints, smudges, and anything stuck on the surface. First, moisten the corner of the cloth. You want to avoid spraying water directly on the screen (phones and water do not mix). Next, use the moistened end to gently wipe up and down the screen. Then, use a dry corner of the cloth to remove any excess moisture from the screen. Repeat on the back surface of the phone, avoiding the camera lens opening if there is one. You want to avoid using coarse or abrasive cloths (including bath towels and paper towels), as these could scratch your screen.

2. **Cotton swabs**. Cotton swabs (like a Q-tip) can help remove dust or tiny crumbs that landed on your phone. You may find a cotton swab works

better than a microfiber cloth for getting hard to reach spots on your phone and does wonders for cleaning out the corners of your cell phone case. They can also prove useful for cleaning out ports.

3. **Avoid alcohol mixtures and harsh chemicals**. If you use an Apple product, remember that Apple does not recommend using any alcohol, ammonia, or other cleaning substances on their products.

You should clean your device regularly (we recommend at least once per day). It is something you can do while watching the evening news or right before bed if you keep your phone by your bedside. Try to clean it as soon as any potentially staining substances land on it like makeup, spilled ink, and so on. Note, however, that these cleaning techniques will remove smears from the display and make it easier to read your device, but they will not remove microorganisms such as bacteria or viruses. See the next tip for information on addressing bacteria and other microorganisms.

SANITIZE YOUR TECH WITH ULTRAVIOLET LIGHT!

Smartphones and tablets collect germs. Some claim that the average device has a comparable bacteria count to a public toilet. If you did not realize this, ultraviolet (UV) light can kill many microorganisms including bacteria, viruses, and protozoa. Reports claim that subjecting your device to a treatment with UV light can kill more than 99 percent of the microorganisms living on it.

We do not know about you, but from where we stand, a device with 99 percent less bacteria and viruses sounds pretty good in terms of helping to protect your health. Additionally, UV does not require transportation, storage, or handling of harmful or corrosive chemicals.

UV light has found acceptance as a sanitizing agent over the past decade or so, even in the medical profession. We have seen UV light devices designed specifically to clean particular devices, such as electric toothbrushes or cell phones. While we like what those devices do, we rarely like those devices as they require you to purchase a new device for each piece of technology. (Note, however, that while they make boxes to hold cell phones, we have not found any that hold laptops or tablets or e-readers.) Our preference (and recommendation) is that you go to a supplier such as Amazon .com and purchase a UV wand. You can use the same wand on many devices, phones, tablets, e-readers, laptops, and so on. We found satisfactory UV wands on Amazon .com for around $20 and up, depending on the size. We chose a battery-powered, folding, pocket-sized wand for easy portability and use for travel.

Once you get one, make it a practice to use it on your devices daily.

Note, however, that while the UV wand will kill microorganisms, it does not clean smears off of the display. You need to do that separately (see the immediately preceding tip).

BLACK LIGHT: IT'S NOT JUST FOR POSTERS

When you hear the term "black light," those of you who came of age in the 1960s will immediately think of the posters we put in dorm rooms that showed to their best advantage illuminated under black light. Those of you who have spent the past 20 years watching crime shows on television have probably learned that black light can illuminate bodily fluids at crime scenes. Black light turns out to be even more versatile; it can also help you spot pockets of bacteria on your electronic devices and urine stains from the family dog on your carpet. We like to take it with us when we travel and give the hotel bed a quick once-over. Suspicious markings may suggest that the hotel did not change the bedspread after someone got caught with his or her pants down; and you may want to ask them to change it for you.

While black light actually is a type of UV light, it differs from the germicidal version of UV light. In its most basic terms, the germicidal version of UV light represents a shortwave UV light, while the black light uses a longwave UV light.

We strongly recommend that you invest a few dollars in a good black light source (we like battery-powered black light flashlights for portability) to help you figure whether you have sufficiently cleaned (or need to clean) your devices. Use it for other purposes, like checking your carpet or illuminating a black light poster if you can find one. You can get very satisfactory handheld black light flashlights on Amazon.com for between $10 and $25. We also found a pair of plastic-framed UV protective safety glasses with a yellow tint on Amazon.com for $6.75. If you wear prescription glasses, here is a bonus: they will likely fit over your regular glasses.

One word of warning, however. Black light can damage your eyes, so do not look directly at it. You would do well to get some tinted glasses that protect your eyes from UV radiation. We like yellow glasses for that purpose as they do not interfere with seeing the pockets of bacteria lit up by the light.

TRAVEL TECHNOLOGY TIPS

TRAVEL TIPS FOR SENIORS

One of the nice things about getting older is that you reach the point where you say, "I have worked long enough, and I need to take more time to enjoy life and to travel instead of work." In truth, you would be well advised to not wait and make time to enjoy life and to travel while you are younger. For those of you who still are young, take heed. For those no longer young, never fear, you still have time; but do not keep putting it off.

While we live in unquestionably troubled times, we have some real advantages over those who lived before us. The world has grown far smaller (a mixed blessing), but once you get past the Transportation Security Administration (TSA), travel has generally become easier and faster (although not always as pleasant as it used to be). One of the nice things about where we find ourselves in time is that technology allows us to work part time, be semi-retired, stay in touch with those at home (family and work), and enjoy traveling as senior attorneys if not senior citizens. With that in mind, we have some suggestions to help you make your travel easier and more fun.

PLAN AHEAD

While traveling as a vagabond holds some appeal, most people seem to have found that it holds less and less appeal as they get older. Most of us generally feel more comfortable if we know where we are going, how we will get there, and where we will stay when we arrive. Travel agents that functioned 40 and 50 years ago by and large no longer exist. Instead of having someone make all our travel arrangements, many of us now make our own. The Internet has become our travel agent and our concierge. Your best bet is to figure out where you want to go, look at some guidebooks to determine what you want to see when you get there, and then contact a consolidator (Expedia.com, Hotels.com, Orbitz.com, and so on) to figure out where to stay. We have found some very nice hotels at very reasonable prices using that approach. You may also find discounted airfares through consolidators. (For those of you wondering how this is a tech tip, remember, you are using the Internet for planning.) Before you look for a hotel, however, think about where you want to stay (in what part of each city). For example, if you enjoy history and want to spend most of your time in an older European city looking around the old town, look for a nice hotel near that part of town. If you do a bit of research you can find accommodations near almost every part of town where you might want to spend a lot of time.

You will also learn to use the Internet to make your reservations for planes, trains, and automobiles, as well as hotels. We have also found that often you can arrange for local tours online and get access to exhibits, sites, museums, and the like through the Internet. Many, if not most, sites that require advanced admission ticket reservations have Internet sites that allow you to make the required arrangements online.

Of course the easiest way to travel sometimes is to sign up for a tour and let the tour company handle the details. Some people genuinely prefer that approach. We prefer doing most of our own planning and taking short half-day or day tours at our destination.

TAKE THE TRAIN

Like Sheldon on the *Big Bang Theory*, we love trains, particularly the ones running in Europe, where they have generally figured out how to make the train system work effectively and efficiently. Trains give you a better chance than planes to see the countryside as you travel, cost less, and involve less hassle than flying. We particularly like them for relatively short day trips and trips between various European cities that only require several hours of travel by train. Taking the train allows us to see the local scenery, snap a few pictures as we go, and either read or do some work along the way. While trains (even the Trans European Express or TEE trains) travel more slowly than planes, you may find it takes less time to get from point A to point B on a train than by plane, particularly on a relatively short trip. (If you wonder how this is a tech tip, think in terms of a good digital camera, an e-reader (Kindle), and a laptop or tablet or smartphone for Internet access while you travel on the train, where such access generally works much better than on a plane.) Note that not all trains have wireless service available and you may need to bring your own cellular connection along with you. In that event, you will likely get service when near a city or large town but lose it when traveling in more rural areas.

The difference in cost for first and second class on a train is far less than the difference in cost for economy and business or first class on a plane, and we have found that the first class accommodations offer a pretty nice and quite comfortable atmosphere. Also, we have never heard of a train company physically dragging passengers off of a train because of a seat shortage.

We are not big fans of overnight travel on a train, as the sleeping compartments come fairly small and you do not get to see much scenery at night, although it certainly beats overnight travel on a plane, unless you spring for first class.

GET YOUR MOBILE DEVICES PROVISIONED FOR INTERNATIONAL USE

Get your cell phone and, if necessary, your tablet, provisioned for international use before you leave. Some plans now offered make it reasonable to use your own phone/tablet and domestic provider in some countries. That is a very new development. As recently as 2017, it still made better sense to buy a SIM card from a local provider at your destination and pop it into an unlocked device, rather than use your domestic provider and incur roaming charges. In 2018, we found much better arrangements available with some providers, particularly for Mexico and Canada. In our opinion, of the domestic providers, AT&T currently has the best packages for international travel, particularly for Mexico and Canada. Be advised, however, that the carriers often modify their plans and that could change at any time.

Before you leave, call your phone service provider and ask about the available international service plans. You will likely find you can make calls but will pay for minutes at a heavily discounted (but still substantial rate). Note that you can also get apps that will allow you to make actual phone calls using a Wi-Fi connection. If you have that facility and available Wi-Fi, the phone calls cost you nothing.

Unless you buy local Internet access, be sure to turn cellular data off on both your mobile phone and your tablet before you arrive in a foreign country. You may be OK just turning off the roaming feature, but why take chances? In addition, buried in your operating system you will likely find a toggle to allow cellular data to assist weak Wi-Fi. You do not want to get caught in that trap, as even if you think you are working on a Wi-Fi connection, if the connection could use some help, your device will seek a mobile connection compatible with your home provider and put it into service to help you out in terms of the connection. As the data charges for those connections tend towards the exorbitant, you do not want to go that route.

Because the location of the toggle for cellular assist appears in different locations on different devices and in different operating systems, we will not try to cover where to look in this tip. Instead, we commend you to your provider's tech support. They can tell you where to look on your device.

USE WI-FI AND TEXT MESSAGING

Most of the international plans we have explored for cell phones include a discount for the per minute calling rate, a miniscule amount of data, and unlimited text messaging. Some newer plans cost more but offer better features.

While some people feel they have to talk on the telephone, in today's world, the smartphone serves as a multimodal communications device. It handles voice calls, video calls, e-mail, and text messaging. If you have not mastered all of these modes, take some time and familiarize yourself with them before you travel. We have found we can handle most of our required communications with the office and the folks at home through text messages (which you can send at any time) and e-mails (which you will only want to send using Wi-Fi to avoid data charges).

USE YOUR MOBILE DEVICE AS A TRAVEL AGENT AND GUIDE

You can find apps and maps galore in the store for your phone. Some are free, some cost a little more. We have found a pretty good collection for a relatively small investment for every place we have traveled in the past several years. In addition to guidebooks, Global Positioning System (GPS)-based map and direction systems, local transit system maps, and local taxi apps are good things to add to your collection.

We like the Lonely Planet guides, Frommer's and Fodor's guides, Tripwolf, and TripAdvisor a lot. In terms of maps and directions, look at Sygic and Ulmon Pro besides Google Maps and the Apple Map program. As your phone will be with you most of the time and most of the contemporary smartphones have GPS functionality, it only makes good sense to keep the apps there and take them with you. There is no harm in putting them on a tablet, but tablets get left in the hotel when phones do not, so make the phone your first choice.

You can do a fair amount of planning by loading guidebooks onto your phone or tablet (or computer) prior to your departure and checking out the details in your spare time before you leave.

You can also use your phone or tablet to make airline reservations, hotel reservations, reservations for dinner, and reservations for a wide variety of tours all over the world. You will find it helpful to add to your arsenal of applications the apps from the major airlines (and regional airlines where you will travel) and hotel and flight consolidators (such as Priceline.com, Orbitz .com, and Expedia.com, among many others). Within the United States (and a few other countries), OpenTable will come in quite handy for restaurant selection and reservations.

GET THE INSIDE SCOOP WITH AIRFAREWATCHDOG.COM

Planning your next trip is always exciting, but trying to find the right airfare and hotel accommodations to fit your budget can get frustrating. That is where travel sites like Airfarewatchdog.com can be useful. Airfarewatchdog.com is a travel site that allows you to set up e-mail alerts for fare deals to destinations of your choice. It was founded in 1998 by George Hobica, a travel journalist with a focus on consumer issues. The site reflects his background well, focusing on many concerns of travelers in devising its search algorithm. The site searches all airlines (although Southwest Airlines is searched selectively). It is not a booking site itself, so when you choose a trip it will direct you to the site to complete your purchase. When you get to the web page, you will find a search and compare feature that allows you to compare an array of sites at once to find the best fare. You can also find the top 50 fares from around the world at that moment. The flexible date search finds the best fares for destinations in the United States and Canada. You can search for the best fares from your departure city, if you are open to where you take your next adventure. You can also sign up for fare alerts for your desired location/dates, and you will be notified by e-mail when the price dips.

The site also provides discounts for hotel reservations, compiling a search of several online booking sites for the lowest price available.

Airfarewatchdog.com actively posts impressive airfare deals on Twitter, so if you are on that social media platform consider following them.

Bonus tip: Sign up for the website's free e-newsletter, *Airfarewatchdog Insider*, for helpful, interesting travel articles.

BRING SOME ENTERTAINMENT

You can add music, movies, books, and lectures to mobile devices. We keep mostly music on the phone and use the tablets for music and video. We prefer using a tablet to the phone for movies due to screen size, but it really is not too bad watching a movie on a phone, particularly one of the larger ones like the Samsung Note or Galaxy or the iPhone 8 or 8 Plus or the X/XS/XS Max. Download the media to your device before you leave, so that you have it on the plane. If you want or need to download more once you leave the United States, make sure you have a good Wi-Fi connection to ensure that it does not cost you a vital organ for the data download.

Do not limit yourself to music and movies. You can get some very high-quality podcasts and even university-quality classes/lectures online. Some come free and others will cost you something, but generally not very much. If you enjoy reading, add a few books to the package. You can put them on a Kindle or add the Kindle app to your phone or tablet. If you would rather just listen to someone tell you a story, check out the options available as audiobooks.

Finally, do not ignore the games section of the App Store/Play Store. You can find some very entertaining games, and some will even stimulate your mind. We like Scrabble a lot; and some of the arcade games will also keep you busy and likely entertained for quite a while.

You will not want to forget to include a good selection of music that you enjoy. Even if you plan on working or reading, you may enjoy some background music.

BUY A BUCKET OF DATA ACCESS

Most providers now sell large data access packages and let you bring multiple devices to the account and share the access. If you get a plan such as this, it makes no difference if you access the Internet on your smartphone, your tablet, or your laptop using a stand-alone cellular hotspot as you will still use the same data access. Most carriers let you augment the plan in the middle of a month if your use exceeds your estimated needs. If you use a plan like this, it may cost an additional $10/month for each tablet or hotspot you add to the account. We consider that a very reasonable amount. Most carriers charge more for adding smartphones, often as much as $35/month. We think that is high, but we pay it anyway as it still generally is the best deal we can get.

Be forewarned, however, that most plans sold by Internet service providers (ISPs) in the United States only work in the United States (some now also work in Canada and/or Mexico) and the rates your ISP charges dramatically increase when you cross the border to any other country. You can, however, purchase data access plans for international use (often at 3G rather than 4G speeds) in the form of cellular hotspots that work internationally. You can also get similar plans from local providers once you are overseas, provided you have compatible or unlocked hardware.

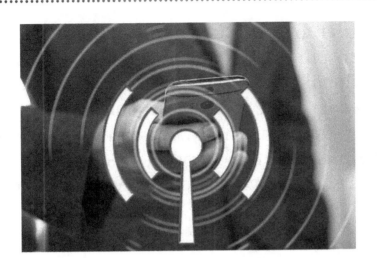

INTERNATIONAL HOTSPOT

The GlocalMe U2 ($119.99, Amazon.com) is a 4G mobile hotspot you can use to have a low-cost Wi-Fi signal anywhere in the world. One of the most unique features is the cloud-SIM technology that allows you to access international data roaming packages with no physical SIM card. You no longer have to pay your cell phone company a daily fee for international use. It offers high-speed 4G Internet with 150 megabits per second (Mbps) download/50 Mbps upload Smart Connect (which will automatically choose the best bandwidth available for you). You can connect up to five devices to this hotspot—pretty much anything that is Wi-Fi-enabled, including iPhones, iPads, tablets, laptops, and smartphones.

You can check e-mail, stream television or news channels, surf the web, and more without limitation. The hotspot is designed with a lightweight and slim profile that can easily fit into a pocket, carry-on bag, or purse. Its metallic satin finish has a nice, modern look.

One of the authors (Ashley) recently tested it during a nine-day visit to Canada, and the device worked flawlessly, allowing both her and her husband to stay connected to loved ones at home whether they were traversing the mountains or urban jungles. Their current cellular provider is AT&T, which offers a $10 International Day pass you can sign up for once you are abroad. Had they used the provider's plan, they would have paid $90 each ($180 total). With the GlocalMe, they paid $119.99 for the device, which came with a one gigabyte (GB) data package. Heavy data users, they bought an additional 1 GB package before the end of the trip (€12, around $14

USD), so for the first trip with this device, their savings was $46. Subsequent trips will have substantially more savings since they will not have the initial cost of the device.

Getting the device set up takes a few steps that we will talk you through. We recommend you set it up and try out the connection before you travel abroad so you can easily work out any kinks without accruing roaming charges on your phone. When you take the device out of the box, it will have some charge, but you should connect the charger to a Universal Serial Bus (USB) power source to get up to a full charge first. When you are ready:

1. Download the GlocalMe app to your smartphone or tablet, open it, and set up an account.
2. Power on the device, and you will see the Wi-Fi symbol (📶) light up with a white light
3. Next you need to register the device in the app. You will notice a black and white QR code (▦) on the back of the hotspot. Go back to the app and select "Register Device" or tap

the "Scan QR Code" symbol (⌐⌐) in the top left corner of your screen. Once you are registered, your free GB will automatically load and you will get a notice when you are close to running out of data. At that point you can buy a package that will last for 30 days or pay as you go.

Now you are powered on, with data loaded and ready to go. The network name and device password are printed on the QR code label for easy reference.

Bonus tip: You can check the battery level of the hotspot by pressing the power button once. You can check the Wi-Fi signal by pressing the same power button twice.

DEALING WITH FOREIGN CURRENT

The United States uses 110 volt (V) electric current as its primary output. We also use 220V current for some appliances, but most of our output lines use the lower voltage. In many countries, 220V–240V comes as the standard output. If you plug a 110V appliance into a 220V outlet, you get to buy a new appliance and, hopefully, do not start a fire. You do not want to do that.

When you travel out of the country, you find that in many places they use plugs with different configurations than those in the United States. That will not come as a surprise to most of you. When you want to use appliances made for the United States in a foreign country that does not use the same configuration as the United States, you need to get either an adapter or a converter (or a combination device that handles both needs). An adapter does not change the power or voltage of the current; it simply allows you to plug your standard U.S. configuration plug into the foreign configuration. That means if you get an adapter and plug a 110V appliance into a 240V you still fry the appliance.

Some of your devices come with chargers or power blocks that accept both 110V and 240V input (many computers, tablets, and smartphones come with such chargers). If you have and use such a charger, the adapter gives you all the help you need to use it in a foreign country. As adapters generally only accept one appliance, that means you can only charge one thing at a time or that you need to bring multiple adapters. You can get power converters that use a single receptacle, with an adaptive plug that comes as part of the set that functions as a multi-outlet power strip using U.S.-compatible plugs. Some also include independent USB ports to allow you to dispense with separate chargers for your USB connective devices and simply plug them into the travel adapter/converter. Most have two or three electric plug receptacles and four USB ports. Some have on/off switches, so you do not have to continually unplug them when not using it. We have found several of these devices available on

Amazon.com as complete kits, including the converter, the adapter plugs, and a carrying case, for prices in the $30–$50 range. We have not tried them all, so we cannot compare them, but we have used and liked the BESTEK offerings and in particular the $42.95 BESTEK Travel Adapter 220V to 110V Voltage Converter with 6A 4 USB Ports and UK/AU/US/EU Plug Adapter.

USE A PERSONAL ELECTRIC VEHICLE

As we age, many of us lose some of our mobility because of illness, injury, or bodily deterioration. We use canes, walkers, and various types of mobility devices ranging from manually propelled wheelchairs to many configurations of electronic scooters, chairs, and so on.

Unfortunately, losing mobility causes many people to travel or even get around town less due to their limitations. That represents a very bad choice in most cases. Science and medicine generally accept that the more active we remain as we age, the more likely we will live longer and age more gracefully. Many who have lost the ability to ambulate with ease choose to stay home rather than try to deal with the rigors of travel compounded by the use of a cane or a walker. Some of the reluctance stems from embarrassment at being hampered and part from the inconvenience of having to move so slowly with a cane or a walker. By way of background, one of the authors (Jeff) has acquired some mobility issues as a result of the fact that he has type 2 diabetes and peripheral neuropathy in his feet. The neuropathy creates some balance issues, which causes him to use a cane and/or an assistance dog when he walks. The neuropathy also causes pressure ulcers on the bottoms of his feet.

In his current state of semiretirement, Jeff has continued to travel frequently. Before he developed neuropathy, he would often walk 15,000 or more steps in a day while traveling, compared to about 3,000 to 5,000 steps at home. The walking while traveling generally resulted in developing pressure ulcers, causing his doctors to tell him to walk less.

To adapt to that limitation and still continue to travel, several years ago, Jeff started renting mobility devices from time to time. As time went on and the problem continued, he bought one to take with him when traveling. These devices go by many names: scooters, mobility devices, motorized chairs, wheelchairs, and, more recently, some manufacturers have referred to them as "personal electric vehicles," likely to get away from the wheelchair concept and to suggest that they may prove useful to those with minor limitations as well as those with more serious issues. (Jeff likes to call them "senior citizens' go-carts.") They come in many configurations, allowing you to choose what works best for you. Some work on two wheels but require you to stand up on them (like the Segway), some look like three- or four-wheeled scooters, and some look like motorized chairs. Some are big, bulky, and do not break down, some break down into pieces for easy transport in a car, and some fold up to fit easily in most cars. Pricing on these vehicles will vary dramatically by manufacturer and the feature set. Many devices can qualify as medical devices. Discuss with your tax preparer whether you can deduct them. A letter from a physician telling you to get one is a good place to start that process.

Here is another tip: if you get tired walking a lot or have other mobility issues, a personal electric vehicle may prove just the right tonic, even if you do not otherwise need assistance walking.

While wonderful for travel, these devices can also smooth your road in day-to-day use. Aside from the fact that people keep reporting that staying active helps keep your mind as well as your body agile, we discovered a collateral benefit while using these devices. People tend to be nicer and more solicitous to those riding one of these vehicles as opposed to someone just walking with a cane. People in crowded situations who might otherwise brush by, stop to help with doors or to offer other assistance. Using one also gives you a very different perspective about handicapped access to public places.

One final comment about these vehicles: they do not go everywhere. Some of your travels will likely include places not friendly to such vehicles. Depending on your personal condition, that may mean you have to avoid that place, or that you walk that day when you go to visit that site. More and more locations have received modifications to make them accessible, but many historic sites have only stairs and no elevators. That does not mean you do not take the vehicle on the trip; it means you take it and use it whenever you can. If you cannot ambulate satisfactorily without one, you just pick something else to visit and avoid the unfriendly locations.

GET A WHILL MODEL Ci PERSONAL ELECTRIC VEHICLE

You have a lot of personal electric vehicles from which to choose. We checked out several and concluded that WHILL makes one of the best devices out there. The Model Ci is not a cheap date. It will cost you about $4,000. But for that price you get a very sophisticated, electrically powered rolling chair capable of traveling at four speeds forward (think of them as fast, normal, slow, and snail's pace) and one in reverse.

The device weighs in at 115 pounds, but easily breaks down into three primary pieces for loading into almost any standard-sized car or sport utility vehicle (a basket that lives under the seat makes a fourth piece). The heaviest piece of the four weighs only 44 pounds if you remove the battery (approximately six pounds), so loading it should not present major difficulties for most people.

The WHILL works on a powerful and virtually silent electric motor powered by a lithium-ion battery capable of moving the device about eight or so miles per charge (depending on the weight it carries and the terrain it travels). As running out of power represents a very bad option, make it a point to carry the charger (and an appropriate adapter if you are traveling out of the country) with you. We also like the idea of investing in a second battery to allow a battery swap on the road without having to stop to charge the device.

The Model Ci looks like (and is) a chair with wheels. It offers great mobility, as it has an extremely short turning radius. The power goes to the rear, so you get a bit more leverage going up a hill. You steer and set the speed by moving a joystick on the right arm rest. For safety, it has a dead man's switch so that if you take your hand off the joystick, the device quickly brakes to a halt. You can disable/enable the device with an optional electronic key that locks it up, making it difficult to steal.

The Model Ci comes with very unusual-looking front tires designed to improve the device's traction—and they work quite well.

The Model Ci has a basket under the seat that will hold most of your personal items;

you can also easily take a standard backpack and put it on the back of the seat to give you additional storage space. The pictures that follow show you what the Model Ci looks like and how it breaks down (note that they do not show the basket, which mounts under the seat and constitutes the fourth piece). You can remove the battery from the heaviest piece, giving you five pieces, but also reducing the weight by about six pounds. The third picture shows you what the front wheels look like.

In our experience, airlines treat the Model Ci the same way that they would treat a wheelchair; they will allow you to ride it up to the entrance of the plane and then take it and store it in the hold for the flight and then return it to you when you get off the plane at the destination. The airlines do not all have the same rules and regulations respecting gate-checking, so you should check with your carrier on how they want to deal with it. Also, we have found that some airlines will let you leave the battery locked in place, while others want you to remove it, put the chair in free-wheel mode, and carry the battery into the cabin with you. Technically, TSA requires you to remove the battery and carry it into the cabin with you as it is a lithium-ion battery. None of the airlines we checked with counted the battery as one of your carry-on items. Because we also carry a spare battery when we travel, we carried both batteries into the cabin with no issue from the airlines.

GET A TRIAXE SPORT ELECTRIC VEHICLE

Our second choice for a personal electric vehicle to make travel a bit easier comes from France. The Triaxe looks like a mobility scooter, not a chair. It has three wheels (two in back and one in the front). It uses a front wheel hub electric motor that draws its power from a lithium-ion battery. It has a steering mechanism much like a bicycle and, in fact, looks like the handlebars on a bike. The Triaxe has two speeds forward (fast and normal) and one in reverse. You switch the speeds and from forward to reverse using switches on the handlebars. Power comes from turning the right handgrip, much as you would on a motorcycle. The Triaxe also has an integrated luggage rack in the back that slides out to accommodate most carry-on and standard-shaped suitcases. That makes things much easier at the airport.

On the disadvantage side, the Triaxe uses a front wheel hub motor and comes up a bit underpowered on inclines. The Triaxe has no deadman's switch, so you have to brake manually using the hand brake that comes with it.

The Triaxe Sport is somewhat more minimalist than the WHILL Model Ci, and it costs significantly less, $2,300. The Triaxe weighs in at 55 pounds. The Triaxe folds down into a very compact package. It will fit in a smaller space than the WHILL Model Ci once compacted, but because it does not break apart, it remains a single piece at 55 pounds when you lift it into the car.

AIRLINE REGULATIONS FOR PASSENGERS CARRYING LITHIUM-ION BATTERIES

From March 1991 through December 2016, the Federal Aviation Administration (FAA) counted 138 incidents involving lithium-ion batteries as cargo or luggage. The agency admits this might not be a complete list, but it includes incidents such as a fire in the overhead bin of a Delta Airlines flight from Honolulu to Atlanta that was traced to a laptop. Another fire occurred in a checked bag during a flight from Newark to San Juan and started with two spare lithium batteries stored in their charging unit.

The FAA does still allow electronics with lithium-ion batteries to fly in checked luggage or carry-on bags. The restrictions refer to spare lithium batteries because of risk of damage while jostling. The concern is that loose batteries could short-circuit—causing extreme heat or even a fire—if they come into contact with keys, coins, tools, or other batteries. The FAA recommends packing loose batteries in their original packaging or a battery case.

The regulations issued by the FAA (https://www.faa.gov/about/office_org /headquarters_offices/ash/ash_programs /hazmat/passenger_info/media/Airline _passengers_and_batteries.pdf) explain that:

> Passengers can carry most consumer-type batteries and portable battery-powered electronic devices for their own personal use in carry-on baggage. Spare batteries must be protected from damage and short circuit. Battery-powered devices must be protected from accidental activation and heat generation.
>
> Batteries allowed in carry-on baggage include
>
> - Dry cell alkaline batteries: typical AA, AAA, C, D, 9-volt, button-sized cells, etc.
> - Dry cell rechargeable batteries: such as Nickel Metal Hydride (NiMH) and Nickel Cadmium (NiCad). For rechargeable lithium ion batteries; see next paragraph.
> - Lithium ion batteries (a.k.a.: rechargeable lithium, lithium polymer, LIPO, secondary lithium). Passengers may carry all consumer-sized lithium ion batteries (up to 100 watt hours per

battery). This size covers AA, AAA, cell phone, PDA, camera, camcorder, hand-held game, tablet, portable drill, and standard laptop computer batteries. The watt hours (Wh) rating is marked on newer lithium ion batteries. External chargers are also considered to be a battery.

With airline approval, devices can contain larger lithium ion batteries (101–160 watt hours per battery), but spares of this size are limited to two batteries in carry-on baggage only. This size covers the largest aftermarket extended-life laptop batteries and most lithium ion batteries for professional-grade audio/visual equipment.

- Lithium metal batteries (a.k.a.: non-rechargeable lithium, primary lithium). These batteries are often used with cameras and other small personal electronics. Consumer-sized batteries (up to 2 grams of lithium per battery) may be carried. This includes all the typical non-rechargeable lithium batteries used in cameras (AA, AAA, 123, CR123A, CR1, CR2, CRV3, CR22, 2CR5, etc.) and the flat round lithium button cells.

Non-spillable wet batteries (absorbed electrolyte) are limited to 12 volts and

100 watt hours per battery. These batteries must be the absorbed electrolyte type (gel cells, AGM, and so on) that meet the requirements of 49 CFR 173.159a(d); i.e., no electrolyte will flow from a cracked battery case. Batteries must be in strong outer packaging or installed in equipment. Passengers are also limited to two (2) spare (uninstalled) batteries. Spare batteries' terminals must be protected (non-conductive caps, tape) within the outer packaging. Batteries and outer packaging must be marked "non-spillable" or "non-spillable battery." Note: This exception is for portable electronic devices, not for vehicle batteries. There are separate exceptions for powered wheelchairs.

With your checked baggage, generally the same rules apply, except for spare (uninstalled) lithium metal and lithium-ion batteries. The FAA regulations elaborate further:

> The batteries must be protected from damage and short circuit or installed in a device. Battery-powered devices— particularly those with moving parts or those that could heat up—must be protected from accidental activation. Spare

lithium metal and lithium ion/polymer batteries are prohibited in checked baggage—this includes external battery packs. Electronic cigarettes and vaporizers are also prohibited in checked baggage. "Checked baggage" includes bags checked at the gate or planeside.

Some specific devices are banned from flights, such as the Samsung Galaxy Note 7, which was banned in October 2016 after nearly 100 reports of the devices overheating and, in some instances, injuring owners.

USING THE INTERNET

Every year, a growing number of seniors embrace the Internet to become more digitally connected. According to a 2017 report from the Pew Research Center, four out of ten seniors now own smartphones, a figure that has doubled since 2013. Internet use has also risen steadily since then. Back in 2000, 14 percent of seniors reported using the Internet. Today that number has grown to 67 percent for adults ages 65 and older. The study reports that once online, most seniors make the Internet a standard part of their daily routine, with roughly three-quarters of senior Internet users going online daily. This demographic is sometimes called the "Silver Surfers." The vast majority of seniors using the Internet do so to communicate with family and friends, and for online shopping. The next most common uses include:

- Gathering health care information or learning about medical issues
- Comparing prices for purchases
- Keeping up with news in the community
- Watching television shows, movies, and other video

This chapter focuses on tips you can use when you go online.

ONLINE LEGAL MARKETPLACES AND THE "UBER-IZATION" OF LEGAL SERVICES

Online legal marketplaces allow potential clients to "shop" for a lawyer without having to schedule initial consultations and spend hours traveling from firm to firm. They address the access to justice problems in America. According to the Justice Index (https://justiceindex.org/) from the National Center for Access to Justice:

> Justice depends on having a fair chance to be heard, regardless of who you are, where you live, or how much money you have. At minimum, a person should be able to learn about her rights and then give effective voice to them in a neutral and nondiscriminatory, formal or informal, process that determines the facts, applies the rule of law, and enforces the result.[2]

In some jurisdictions, more than 80 percent of the civil legal needs of lower-to-middle

---

2. *Measuring Access to Justice*, THE JUSTICE INDEX 2016, https://justiceindex.org/ (last accessed July 19, 2018).

income individuals goes unmet for obvious reasons: lawsuits and attorneys are expensive. This prompted the emergence of unregulated online legal service providers (e.g., LegalZoom.com, LawDepot.com, RocketLawyer.com) and online legal marketplaces (e.g., Avvo.com, MontageLegal .com, HireAnEsquire.com).

The online legal marketplace connects individuals with lawyers for a reduced-fee consultation to give individuals some guidance on what they can do to address their legal needs. Some marketplaces offer fixed fees for unbundled (limited-scope) services. This allows potential clients access to services at a more comfortable price point, and knowledge of exactly what they are getting in exchange for what they pay. For attorneys, online legal marketplaces may sound appealing because they allow you access to potential clients, and a way to compete with do-it-yourself legal sites. This type of service also addresses some of the common headaches in running a law practice: getting clients, billing, and getting paid. You need to be wary of these services and how they are looked upon in

your state. Participating in an online marketplace could be an ethics violation. Some
states have issued ethics opinions about
whether attorneys using a program like
an online legal marketplace would violate
the rules that prohibit fee sharing with
non-lawyers, among other rules.

USE THE INTERNET TO PLAN YOUR NEXT ACTIVITY

If you and the members of your social group are ready to get out of the house, here are some websites to help you plan what to do next:

- **Find a new restaurant to try on Yelp.com**. Yelp is a website founded in 2004 to help people search for local businesses. It has grown into an excellent source for finding reviews and suggestions of restaurants for anywhere you live or travel. Besides finding reviews of businesses and restaurants, you can use Yelp to find local events, top ten favorite lists, and even talk with other Yelpers (Yelp users). If you like the idea of trying a new place but do not relish waiting for a table, call the restaurant for a reservation ahead of time, or check out **OpenTable.com** to see if you can make a reservation online.

- **Find a movie on Rotten Tomatoes.com**. Rotten Tomatoes measures the quality of movies and television shows with its measure, the Tomatometer. It accumulates the reviews for a movie and measures the percentage that is more positive than negative. It then assigns an overall fresh or rotten rating to the film. If the movie scores above 60 percent, it is considered fresh, whereas scores of 59 percent and below are considered rotten.

- **Plan to hit the open road with Roadtrippers.com**. Roadtrippers is one of the fastest-growing web and mobile travel planning platforms. This unique website will guide you "off the beaten path" with places to visit and interesting locations. You can use the site to plan a route, book a hotel, and explore interesting places along the way. Atlas, part of the Roadtrippers.com platform, is a robust, comprehensive location database for travel and tourism. Atlas categorizes locations to assist users in finding places that interest them.

- **Find local events on Facebook**. You can explore local events to find one that sounds interesting and fits your schedule. From the Facebook home screen, you will find a menu of links on the left side of the screen, labeled "Explore." Under that, you will see a link to "Events." Click the link and you will find upcoming events that you have been invited to by your friends and contacts, along with suggested events from Facebook's algorithm based on your likes and interests. On the right side of the screen you will find a list of your friends' upcoming birthdays (a helpful reminder if you would like to send a card or friendly note). You will also find events popular with your friends, and a note of anyone on your contact list interested in attending it.

USE THE INTERNET TO MANAGE YOUR FINANCES

Whether you are approaching retirement or already enjoying it, your financial situation will look different than before. Managing your finances can become more difficult as time goes on, and you could struggle to stay on top of bills and follow a monthly budget. Many online tools can help make managing your finances easier, including:

- **Create a monthly budget and track your spending with Budget pulse.com**. Budgetpulse offers free budget planning, personal finance software. You can organize your cash flow, expenses, and bank accounts in one place. Many online personal finance managers are designed for you to input your username and password to link your accounts to their system. If this idea makes you uncomfortable then you will like Budgetpulse.com. This site lets you import the information from your financial institution manually, allowing you to limit who can access your accounts.

- **Create a budget quickly and easily with BudgetSimple.com**. BudgetSimple is a free and easy to use online budget planner. It employs a proven method of budgeting to help you track your spending. The website will analyze your finances, help you plan a budget, and make suggestions where you can cut expenses or grow your savings. With the free account you can manually import reports from your financial institution. If you want the ease of linking your accounts and use of their mobile app, you must subscribe to the Plus service ($4.99/month).

- **Give your finances a physical at EconomicCheckUp.org**. EconomicCheckUp is a web resource provided by the National Council on Aging. The website will customize the resources based on some basic information you provide for it. It includes calculators to help you create a budget, plan your retirement spending, and find ways to cut your expenditures. The website will also direct you to any government resources where you may qualify for assistance that will help increase your income for retirement or save on your main expenses.

- **Master your financial picture with Mint.com**. Mint is one of the most popular personal financial management tools on the web today. It is easy to use and offers a lot of tools to help you stay on top of your finances. It is designed for you to link your financial accounts to it, and if you are comfortable with this then it has a lot to offer. It will analyze your personal habits and help you create and stick to a budget based on your priorities. Mint brings all your accounts and bills into one place, so you can manage everything from the one log-in. You can set up alerts so you get a message any time a bill is close to being due or if your funds are low, even if you do not think to log in. As an added bonus, you can check your credit score easily on the website and get alerted whenever particularly large charges occur, as this is sometimes a sign of identity theft.

- **Set up Internet access for your bank accounts.** You can set up Internet access for checking, savings, credit, and other accounts at most banks. Many have apps for smartphones and tablets. These applications generally allow you to check balances, pay bills electronically and/or automatically from anywhere in the world, and even deposit checks without ever going near a bank or automatic teller machine (ATM).

USE THE INTERNET TO STAY SOCIALLY ACTIVE

A study published in the *Journal of Health and Social Behavior* found that older adults with high or medium levels of engagement that increased over time developed cognitive and physical limitations more slowly than did those with low levels of engagement that decreased over time. Some observed that the more socially isolated seniors visit a doctor's office much more often than their socially active peers. Social interaction looks different depending on your personality, and one idea will not fit everyone. For some, it may be going out with family; others prefer their social circle of friends. Some may relish the idea of touring a new place with a group of strangers who may turn into new friends by the end. For others, this may be too much "new" to stomach. You can use the Internet to find ideas for social interaction comfortable for you. Other benefits of staying socially active include:

- Reduced risk for mental health issues (including depression and poor cognitive function)
- More physical activity during social activities
- A more stable support system
- Positive impact on overall mood and self-esteem

If you are looking for ideas to stay socially active:

- **Start by reaching out to friends and family**. You can do this by phone, e-mail, or social media. The top social media sites online are Facebook, YouTube, Instagram, Twitter, Reddit, and Pinterest. We covered setting up accounts on most of these social media sites in our previous tips book.
- **Find groups with similar interests through Meetup.com**. Meetup is a website designed to help people find local communities that meet offline about their shared interests and passions.

Some groups stay physically active, explore the city, read books, tour craft breweries, expand professional networks, or pursue many activities and interests. Meetup makes it easier to try something new and meet new people. You get the comfort of knowing that when you go out, you will meet someone with the same exact goal as you, who is looking for you and expecting you to be there. Successful meetups are a welcoming and friendly environment and a great way to expand your social activity.

- **Find Facebook groups that align with your interests**. On the left side of the Facebook home page, there is a menu titled "Explore." Under it you will see a link to "Facebook Groups." Click this link and at first you will see groups you are a part of and groups you have been invited to join. At the top of the page there is a link titled "Discover"; select that one and you can look for groups with which you share a common interest. Facebook will try to help by recommending groups based on your location, the posts you like, or groups you have already joined. There is also a section where you can see groups that your friends and contacts have joined. You will also see recommendations for local groups, businesses, professional networking groups, style, sports, parenting, travel, home and garden, and more.

- **Check out the AARP online community**. AARP hosts an online community with organized discussion topics. Don't see something that interests you? You can start the conversation with a topic of your own.

USE THE INTERNET TO TRAIN YOUR BRAIN

You may have heard the phrase "brain training" in the past and wondered what it is, why it is helpful, and how one goes about training. Brain training grew out of the scientific studies on neuroplasticity, or brain plasticity. Brain plasticity refers to the brain's natural ability to remodel itself throughout a lifetime. The brain is constantly changing—sometimes in a good way and sometimes not. Studies indicate the brain feels the effects of aging as early as 30 (so even the younger of the two authors is affected by this). There are certain activities, games, and exercises you can do to keep your brain healthy and active, no matter your physical condition. Here are some websites that offer suggestions or games that can improve your cognitive performance:

- **Read the articles or play games on SeniorBrains.com**. Senior-Brains.com offers brain fitness for seniors, including free brain exercises, puzzles, games, and training for anyone over 50.

- **Get rigorous training for your brain at BrainHQ.com**. BrainHQ is an online brain-training system that stems from more than 30 years of research in neurological science. You can sign up for free exercises or subscribe for full access (subscriptions are $14/month, or $8/month if you pay for an annual subscription). Each level of training exercises takes no more than five minutes, making it one of the fastest workouts you can do and benefit from.

- **Get mentally fit with Lumosity .com**. Lumosity has been around a while and offers a well-developed brain training and mental fitness resource. You can sign up for the free account, which grants you access to three games per day. A subscription service offers unlimited access. Both the free and subscription accounts allow you to track your results and monitor improvement. The service is available on the web or via the downloadable iOS and Android apps.

- **Focus independently on different brain areas with Happy-Neuron.com**. Happy Neuron provides games and activities categorized and divided into five critical brain areas: memory, attention, language, executive functions, and visual/spatial skills. Like Lumosity, it will personalize the training to fit you and track your progress.

- **Play Scrabble, Words with Friends, or word search**. Games like Scrabble or the derivative Words with Friends enable you to interact with the computer at different skill levels and to interact with a wide variety of real people to test your knowledge of words and your ability to assemble them from a selection of letters. It can occupy idle hours, keep you entertained, and keep your mind active, all while helping you improve your vocabulary. Word search games give a different approach to keeping your mind active; they force you to use your recognition skills to find words buried in an apparently random collection of letters. You can find these words with greater or less difficulty depending on your skill level.

- **Last, but certainly not least, the old-fashioned crossword puzzle**. Crossword puzzles are a classic brain trainer, improving both verbal language skills and memory skills over time. Best of all, they are readily available. You will often find them in the newspapers and magazines you read. You can also find a collection of large print crossword puzzles online from Q.E.T.S. (go to http://www.qets.com/crossword_puzzles.htm). Every month the site provides new puzzles you can download for free.

USE THE INTERNET
TO SHOP SMARTER

By 2016, studies indicated that a tide was turning for consumers: shoppers were buying more things online than in stores. The biggest game changer for shoppers was Amazon.com. A study from Business Insider stated in 2015 that one-in-four mobile shoppers (consumers who purchase items or services from their mobile phones) is over the age of 55. On December 19, 2016, the Pew Research Center issued a study on online shopping and e-commerce, indicating that around eight-in-ten Americans are online shoppers, with around 15 percent making online purchases weekly and 28 percent doing so a few times a month.

Why do people prefer online shopping? One of the major conveniences is the ability to get online reviews and ratings about an item before you purchase it. How often have you walked down a store aisle, not confident about which brand or model to buy? Eighty-two percent of the Pew study respondents reported consulting the online reviews before buying something for the first time. Another advantage to online shopping is the ability to compare prices. Trying to get the best deal is a lot more cumbersome if you are driving around from store to store.

If you have not embraced online shopping and are hesitant to do so, we recommend you consider using the Internet on your phone to research a product while you are in the store, especially before a major purchase. If you are open to online shopping, or are already a savvy online shopper, here are a few of our favorite places to shop online:

In general:

- **Amazon.com**. You have probably noticed a lot of the tech we recommend is available from this online retailer. That is because whatever you are looking for, Amazon probably has it. Often you can buy it direct from the manufacturer or major retailers, but you may find lower prices here. Initially, Amazon sold books; today it is the world's largest online retailer of just about everything. The driving force behind Amazon's success is its Prime subscription, a service that offers two-day free shipping on eligible items, and even two-hour "Prime Now" delivery in certain cities. If you want even more savings, check out Amazon's Warehouse Deals (you can select it from the menu to the left of the search bar at the top of Amazon .com's home page).

- **eBay.com**. Founded in 1995 (as AuctionWeb), eBay is a multinational e-commerce site that provides consumer-to-consumer and business-to-consumer sales opportunities in the form of auctions or direct purchase transactions ("buy it now" shopping). It is also a marketplace for online event ticket trading (through StubHub) and textbooks (via Half.com), in addition to other services. When shopping on eBay.com, it is worth knowing that you can filter your search results to show you only items for auction (if you like the sport of bidding), or items that are "buy it now" (allowing you to purchase for the amount designated by the seller), or items that allow you to make a private counteroffer to the seller.

Office supplies:

- **Target.com**. This is the online retail site for the second largest discount store retailer in the United States.
- **OfficeDepot.com**. Office Depot, Inc., owner of both Office Depot and Office Max, is one of the leading providers of business supplies, products, and technology solutions. If you have one close by, you can save time and money by choosing free in-store pick up, when available for your purchase.
- **OfficeSupply.com**. This site offers good prices, along with numerous coupon codes and rebates, freebies, weekly deals, and more.

- **OfficeFurniture2Go.com**. This site offers reasonable prices on nice office furniture and free shipping. Furniture bought through the website comes with a lifetime warranty.

Computers and electronics:

- **Frys.com**. Fry's has a reputation for offering a high level of support for customers, something that may come in useful if the technology you are purchasing is one with which you are not familiar.
- **BestBuy.com**. The electronics retailer offers many of the same deals and more through its website. You can also often find favorable financing terms for your costlier purchases.
- **Newegg.com**. Newegg offers competitive prices on computers, laptops, electronics, televisions, digital cameras, cell phones, and more. The site offers deeper discounts in the form of daily deals.

Grocery shopping:

- **Walmart.com**. Walmart announced in April 2018 that it will offer online grocery delivery to more than 40 percent of U.S. homes through a partnership with Postmates, an on-demand delivery service that launched in 2011. There will be a $30 minimum order and a $9.95 fee for delivery, but this will get you same-day delivery. Walmart also offers a service to allow customers to order groceries online and pick them up at the curb outside the store.

- **Amazon.com**. We discussed them earlier, but it is worth noting that AmazonFresh Grocery will deliver food to you and you can subscribe for routine deliveries or use a dash button that you press whenever you see an item getting low and it will automatically order a replacement based on the last time you ordered the item.

- **Safeway.com**. Safeway offers online grocery shopping with low shipping fees. You can also provide personal instructions to your shopper through the "Request to Personal Shopper" feature. You can make requests like "please provide firm tomatoes" or whatever you prefer.

USE THE INTERNET
TO CELEBRATE MILESTONES

Have you ever suddenly realized that someone important to you has a holiday or anniversary coming up and you forgot to send a card? You could dash out of your nice warm house, get in the car and drive to a local store, pick up a card, fill it out, and take it to a post office for mailing.

Or. . . you could just log onto one of these websites and have their service mail a card out for you.:

- **Postable.com**. Postable will print, stuff, address, and mail all of your cards directly to everyone for you. Need to send 100 thank you cards? Just upload the list and they will take care of it for you. The cards arrive to your intended recipients looking like you wrote them by hand (shhhh . . . we won't tell anyone).

- **Sent-Well.com**. Like Postable, Sent-Well offers handwriting and card mailing services with a beautiful selection of greeting cards, thank you notes, and gifts you can include in your mailings. You can also sign up for occasion reminders and never worry about missing someone's big day.

- **TheGreetingCardShop.com**. This site offers all cards for $1.99 with free personalization. These cards are printed out after you customize them, so they are not handwritten like the prior two sites, but certainly worth the savings for anyone you want to send a card to that is less personal.

USE THE INTERNET FOR YOUR HEALTH AND FITNESS

Good health is one of life's greatest blessings. There are many reasons people tend to slow down with age. Sometimes it is due to health problems, or weight or pain management issues, or even balance issues and the fear of falling. As we age, an active lifestyle becomes even more important. Staying active, within your comfortable range, can:

- Boost your energy
- Maintain your independent lifestyle
- Protect your heart
- Manage pain symptoms, range of motion, and weight issues

It is never too late to start maintaining this gift and there are plenty of websites to help you do that. You can join a gym, sign up for a fitness class, or take a hike. Here are several places to check out if you are ready to get started:

- **If your health insurance participates, take advantage of SilverSneakers.com**. SilverSneakers is a free fitness program for seniors that helps millions of people on Medicare rise up and meet challenges. Membership includes access to every participating gym in their network (which currently consists of more than 14,000 locations). These gyms often have weights, cardio equipment (like treadmills and ellipticals), swimming pools, and other amenities you can use. You can sign up for local fitness classes and find new friends in your area interested in the same activities.

- **Plan your meals and eat healthier on EatThisMuch.com**. EatThisMuch.com is a web-based service focused on providing users tools and support to take control of nutrition. Their tools help you with planning meals, shopping for what you need, and cooking.

- **Track your calorie intake and activity on MyFitnessPal.com.** MyFitnessPal.com offers a wealth of tools, support, and motivation to help you reach fitness goals and eat better. Tracking what you eat is helpful to monitor your sodium, sugar, or fat intake and to see if your diet is missing any vital nutrients. You can also track your caffeine and water intake. You can connect with friends on MyFitnessPal.com, adding another layer of support. Another similar site, LoseIt.com, will also help you keep track of your calories, the proportions of protein, fat, and carbohydrates you consume, your fluid intake, your weight, and sleep patterns. Best of all, it integrates with Fitbit.com and using a Fitbit tracker, which we highly recommend. You wear the Fitbit on your wrist and the tracker records your activities (especially exercise); it also records and evaluates the quality of your sleep.

The information syncs to your online account through your mobile phone or computer and the website can transfer information to and from a multitude of other health-related applications.

- **Get help working toward your fitness goals with Go4Life.** Go4Life (https://go4life.nia.nih .gov/) is a website developed by the National Institute on Aging, part of the National Institutes of Health. The website offers free fitness and nutrition guides, fitness tracking, downloadable reports to monitor your progress, and online virtual coaches to motivate you along the way. They offer suggestions to build endurance, strength, balance, and flexibility no matter what level you are starting at.
- **Get ideas and learn what works from SeniorFitness.com.** At SeniorFitness.com, the goal is simple: avoid the process of falling apart and dying for as long as possible. The website provides

reports on strategies that postpone the loss of mobility and strength, aches and pains, depression, and the chronic disease conditions normally associated with aging. For example, one report revealed that protein requirements increase with age, a counterintuitive idea when you often hear how older adults do not need as many calories overall.

- **Learn how to eat and more with HowStuffWorks.com.** HowStuffWorks.com features a section on diet and aging. One discussion in the section centers on how to eat right as a senior. It includes links to several helpful resources, including **ChooseMy Plate.gov** (where you can customize their nutrition advice according to age, sex, and activity level), a food guide pyramid developed by Tufts University Human Nutrition Research Center on Aging, specific for people age 70 and

older (available at http://hnrca
.tufts.edu/myplate/), and guidance
on meeting the mineral requirements that grow more important
as we age.

USE THE INTERNET TO FIND YOUR NEXT FAVORITE BOOK

Reading is a great hobby to keep you mentally active and engaged. Reading allows you to slip away from the stress in your present life. There is a quote from *A Dance with Dragons*, by George R.R. Martin, where one character explains, "A reader lives a thousand lives before he dies . . . [t]he man who never reads lives only one." The mental stimulation you get from reading can slow down the spread of Alzheimer's and dementia. There are the more

obvious benefits of increasing your knowledge on a subject and expanding your
vocabulary—it is never too late to learn a
new word. Some technology tools that can
improve your reading experience include:

- **Goodreads.com.** Goodreads
  .com is vast site devoted to helping users find and share books
  they love. There is a social ele-
  ment to the site: you can connect
  your Facebook account and if any
  of your friends are users then you
  can see what books they are reading. You can keep a log of books
  you are reading, have read, or
  want to read in the future. Once
  you have given ratings to enough
  books for the website to understand your preferences, it will
  make recommendations based on
  how you rated read books and
  the genres you prefer to read. If
  you are deciding whether to try a
  new author or series, you can read
  other users' reviews of the book to
  see if it is the right fit.

- **Audible.com**. Audible.com has a collection of 45,000 books professionally narrated for your listening enjoyment. A monthly subscription runs around $14.95/month, which gives you one credit per month (most books cost one credit to download). You can sign up for a 30-day free trial and receive two credits to put towards downloads in the first month. Audible offers a "Great Listen Guarantee"; if you are not satisfied with your choice then you can return the audiobook for another title up to one year after purchase. Some books on Audible.com may cost less than $14.95 to download. Since you must pay $14.95 for the Audible membership to get one credit, we recommend you not spend your credits on these books if you want to maximize the value of your credits. If you do not spend your credit for the month, it will roll over, but you can only bank some credits this way.

- **BookBub.com**. BookBub.com alerts users to e-book deals on their favorite authors or books in their preferred genre. It is an easy, fun, and inexpensive way to expand your digital library and discover new authors. When you sign up, you select authors and genres you like, and Book-Bub's editorial team will e-mail you recommendations on sale or deeply discounted. The books run the spectrum from bestsellers to new authors to hidden gems. The books are available from Amazon's Kindle store, Barnes & Noble's Nook store, Apple iBook, and more. BookBub will also notify you about discounts, new releases, and preorders for your favorite authors. You can add or update your favorite author or genre lists anytime from their website.

- **OverDrive.com**. Check if your local library offers a subscription to OverDrive.com. OverDrive is

a free service offered by libraries that lets you borrow digital content (including e-books
and audiobooks) anytime. Each
library chooses the digital content
it wants for their users, making
each collection unique. You must
have an active library card to use
the service, but the convenience
is worth the hassle. No more
late fees or trips to the library to
return your books.

- **HooplaDigital.com**. Hoopla is an
online streaming service for public libraries, like OverDrive.com.
Besides e-books and audiobooks,
Hoopla offers users access to feature films, documentaries, and
music albums. Like OverDrive,
you will need a library card to
access media on Hoopla, but the
content is always available. (Over-
Drive provides a limited number
of licenses per library, meaning
sometimes you have to be on a
waitlist to download a book.)

And do not forget that technology offers you a great way to read (or listen to) your next book selection. You can get one of many available e-readers to use (we do not buy hardbound or paperback books anymore). Carrying an e-reader makes a lot more sense, as you can carry one or many for the same weight and size and you have no storage problem because of buying more books than you have room for at home. Of all the e-readers out there, we like the Kindle Oasis 2 the best. Kindle, as a general rule, has the best e-readers in our opinion. You can also get apps for mobile phones and tablets that make them function like one of many e-readers and use those devices instead of a dedicated e-reader.

No traveler should leave home without an e-reader. For that matter, we seldom leave home for any reason without one in our pockets. They come in handy on public transportation or while waiting in a doctor's office or in a long line at a store.

USE THE INTERNET TO STAY INFORMED

According to *U.S. News*, baby boomers spend an average of 81 minutes a day reading, listening to, or watching the news. The most popular sources for news include newspapers, radio, television, and online. Retirees spend even more time, with an average of 83 minutes a day spent gathering the news from various sources.

Nearly half the population of baby boomers (46 percent) goes online for news at least three days a week, and 33 percent of baby boomers use search engines to find it. But online news is not as popular for older seniors, only 22 percent of whom read online news regularly. With devices that can enlarge font and make carrying your news source lighter and easier though, it may be time to consider getting your news online. If you are interested, here are some sources:

Newspaper Websites

New York Times	NYTimes.com
Washington Post	WashingtonPost.com
USA Today	USAToday.com
Wall Street Journal	WSJ.com
Los Angeles Times	LATimes.com
New York Daily News	NYDailyNews.com
New York Post	NYPost.com
Boston Globe	Boston.com
San Francisco Chronicle	SFGate.com
Chicago Tribune	ChicagoTribune.com
British Daily Mail	DailyMail.co.uk

Broadcast Network Television Websites

MSNBC	MSNBC.com
CNN	CNN.com
ABC News	ABCNews.go.com
Fox News	FoxNews.com
CBS News	CBSNews.com
BBC News	BBC.co.uk

Hybrid Online-Only Sites and News Aggregators

Yahoo News	Yahoo.com/news
AOL News	AOL.com/news
Huffington Post	HuffingtonPost.com
Google News	News.Google.com
Topix	Topix.com
Bing News	Bing.com/news

If you find your preferred news source online, you may want to set that as your home page. That way you can be informed of the latest news stories every time you open up your web browser.

WHERE DO I FIND THE DARK WEB (AND DO I WANT TO FIND IT?)

Lately we have heard lots of talk about something called the "Dark Web." The comments about the Dark Web make it sound rather ominous and, perhaps, rightly so. The Dark Web represents an area where angels rarely tread. Even Google tends to stay away (Google reportedly does not track or search the Dark Web). We believe that to be true, as anecdotal information supports it since we do not know of anyone who has done a Google search and received returns inclusive of the Dark Web. Generally speaking, the Dark Web overlays the Internet, but requires specialized software configurations and/or authorizations to access (you will not get there with your standard browser). If you really want to get there, you need to get a Tor browser and install it on your computer. It comes as a free download.

Once you install it, you can access the Dark Web using the Tor browser.

The term "Dark Web," in general parlance, refers to the seamier side of the web—the place, for example, where stolen identity information gets sold off in wholesale lots. Many users of the Dark Web go there using the anonymity it offers to facilitate illegal acts (including without limitation: drug transactions, stolen identity information sales and purchases, counterfeit goods, weapons, and so on). Because of the illegality of many transactions conducted in the Dark Web, authorities have endeavored to track Dark Web usage and identify Dark Web users.

Not everything sold on the Dark Web is illegal; but you should know that most Dark Web purchases do not get made with Mastercards or Visa cards. Most get handled using cryptocurrencies (such as Bitcoin). FYI, you certainly do NOT want to provide your credit card information to anyone on the Dark Web.

While you may have some curiosity about accessing the Dark Web, we do not recommend it. Centuries ago cartographers used to mark unknown areas as dangerous by noting that "THERE BE DRAGONS HERE" (or words to that effect). Think of the Dark Web as one of those areas. We recommend letting discretion rule and staying away from the Dark Web. If you want to know more about the Dark Web, you can read the information on the Dark Web News (https://darkwebnews.com/). You might find the following particularly interesting in that regard: https://darkwebnews .com/help-advice/access-dark-web/.

TECHNOLOGY AND HOBBY TIPS

GET A HOBBY!

It is important for seniors to have hobbies and leisure activities. Not only are hobbies fun, they can also be a way to refresh the mind and body, aiding you in staying healthy and active. Actively pursuing hobbies and leisure activities can:

- **Reduce stress**. This assumes that whatever your hobby is, it is something you enjoy doing. If it is not, then pick another hobby; there are plenty from which to choose. Hobbies give you a way to take your mind off the stresses of daily life. Some hobbies known for creating a calm atmosphere and reducing stress include cooking or baking, gardening, walking, singing, reading, or playing an instrument.

- **Improve memory**. Many hobbies are challenging, enhancing your problem-solving skills. Hobbies that offer this benefit include word searches, crossword puzzles, brain games (discussed in the

Using the Internet chapter of this book), Sudoku, and card games.

- **Improve flexibility**. Any amount of moving can assist in stretching muscles and improving your range of motion. Some hobbies that improve your flexibility include Wii games, walking, yoga, stretching, swimming, painting, Tai Chi, or dancing.
- **Improve self-esteem**. Some hobbies involve interacting with other people, which creates opportunities to socialize and can improve your self-esteem. The confidence you gain from having a hobby can then prepare you to take on new challenges at work. Hobbies known to be social and improve self-esteem include card games (bridge club, poker, and so on), scrapbooking, board games, shopping, and knitting.
- **Improve sleep quality**. Being active during the day can lead to more restful sleep at night. You will want to do your more active hobbies earlier in the day so you

can be sure to have enough time to wind down before bed.

- **Enhance the immune system**. Physical activity is great for improving your overall immune system. Some physically active hobbies include playing games, horseshoes, golf, bike riding, or basketball.

Mental and social activities are just as vital as physical activity. This chapter will look at some of the technology tools that can improve your experience with hobbies you already enjoy, or help you try new ones.

TECH TOOLS FOR COOKING

Cooking is a hobby one can pick up at any time and enjoy for a lifetime. One obvious benefit of cooking is getting to enjoy the delicious results, but more than that, it keeps your brain active and healthy by requiring you to measure materials, read recipes, and more. Cooking can be a social activity, especially when preparing a meal with children and grandchildren. Here are some high-tech tools for the kitchen:

- **iDevices Kitchen Thermometer** ($39.99, Amazon.com). This dual-probe digital meat thermometer will alert you when your food reaches an optimal temperature, negating the need to hover over the oven. The device will send push notifications to your phone, notifying you of the meat's doneness. It communicates via Bluetooth though, not Wi-Fi, so you will need to be within a 150-foot range to receive the notifications. It is powered by AA batteries, and should have around a 150-hour battery life.

- **Instant Pot Duo Plus60 9-in-1 Multi-Use Programmable Pressure Cooker, Six Quart** ($129.95, Williams-Sonoma.com). This device is the kitchen-version of a Swiss Army knife. It can perform the functions of nine kitchen devices (potentially saving you countertop space) including pressure cooker, slow cooker, rice cooker, steamer, sauté and brown, cake maker, yogurt maker, sterilizer, and warmer. It is preprogrammed with 15 smart programs for soup/broth, meat/stew, bean/chili, cake, egg, slow cook, sauté, rice, multi-grain, porridge, steam, sterilize, yogurt, keep warm, and pressure cook. It is another Bluetooth-enabled device that communicates with an app. The app has a recipe database and allows you to start and stop different functions, so long as you are within a 30- to 45-foot range of the device.

- **ANOVA Precision Sous Vide Cooker** ($108.99, Amazon.com). Sous Vide (pronounced "sue veed") is the process of sealing food in an airtight container (like a vacuum sealed bag), and then cooking that food in temperature-controlled water. You vacuum seal your protein (fish, steak, and so on) along with marinade, sauce, herbs, or spices, and then drop it in a large pot of water. Though the water is heated, it never comes to a boil. The Sous Vide Cooker uses a heated metal coil to warm water to a constant temperature, with no fluctuating between high or low. The cooking process is slow, but precise. Proteins like steak, pork, chicken, and fish will cook for long periods of time, heating up slowly until the entire piece of meat is the same temperature as the water. For example, a 12 ounce New York strip will take a little more than two hours to cook. Once your meat has reached the correct temperature, you will want to finish it off with a little searing on the outside (since the meat is cooked at a low temperature without contact with a hot surface, it does not have the opportunity to get that crisp, caramelized exterior). Heat up a cast-iron skillet and you can sear the meat for a minute on each side (including the small sides), to develop the caramelization without cooking the interior any further.

- **Drop Scale** ($54.99, Amazon .com). This scale from Drop will connect to a companion app to guide you through recipes on your iPhone or iPad. If you do not use exact measurements in baking, your pie or cake could turn into a cooking disaster. You can tell the app if you want to double the recipe and it will adjust the instructions. It will even adjust for you if you use too much of one ingredient or need to substitute for another.

- **CTA Digital Kitchen Mount Stand** ($28.99, Amazon.com). This tablet stand is easy to install in your kitchen. It is adjustable to hold tablets between six inches and 8.75 inches wide and designed to fold out of the way for compact storage. It can display your tablet at any angle, with a 360-degree rotatable mount.

LEARN A FOREIGN LANGUAGE

If you find yourself with some free time, you should really consider learning a foreign language. Learning a new language can improve brain function, enhance personal confidence, and broaden your opportunities for communication and meeting new people. Additional benefits to learning a new language include:

- **Sharpen your decision-making skills**. A study by psychologists at the University of Chicago indicated that when people use a language different from their native tongue, it eliminates the tendency toward loss aversion. Loss aversion is our human impulse to get caught up in the "here and now" instead of making decisions that could become helpful in the future. People tend to react with less emotion when hearing statements in their second language. So it is possible that learning a second language could lead to secondary benefits like better financial decisions, self-control, and an improved ability to retain focus and overall make good decisions.

- **Boost your brain power**. Seniors need to find new ways of learning to increase brain strength and agility. A 2004 study from the University College London examined the brains of 105 people, 80 of whom were bilingual. The research showed that learning a foreign language altered the brain's grey matter, the part of the brain responsible for processing information. This would suggest that people who are bilingual have an easier time understanding new information than those who are monolingual.

- **Broaden your travel horizons**. You will feel more comfortable traveling to a foreign place when you understand the native language. By understanding the native tongue of your destination, you can better learn about the destination's culture and people. It makes interacting with locals easier and more enjoyable.
- **Stave off Alzheimer's and dementia**. Learning another language as an older adult has a great impact on the development and perseverance of the brain. Knowing another language can help protect against the type of cognitive decline that leads to Alzheimer's disease and dementia.

If you want to learn a new language, but are not sure which one you will like, then you can try a few out with the free online/ application Duolingo (discussed more in

"Jeff's Favorite Apps" in the chapter Jeff's and Ashley's Favorite Apps). If you know which language you would like to learn, Rosetta Stone has dominated the market for online language learning programs for a while now. There are also a few others you can try, like Memrise (free, iOS/Android), busuu (free, iOS/Android), AccelaStudy Essential apps (free, iOS), or 24/7 Tutor apps (free, iOS).

TECHNOLOGY FOR THE GARDENER

Gardening is a hobby with many benefits for seniors, including improving endurance and strength, and reducing stress levels. Edible gardening has even more benefits. One of the nice things about gardening is that the tools and environment can be modified to accommodate physical limitations. The physical activity qualifies gardening as a form of exercise. Outdoor gardening increases your exposure to sunlight, which causes your body to produce more vitamin D. This promotes healthier bones, mood, and sleep. However, it is important to take in sunlight in moderation, to avoid overexposure and sunburn.

If you are an avid gardener, or considering picking the hobby up, here are some technology tools you may want to check out:

- **Plant sensors**. Plant sensors are devices you can put in the soil to gather information on the growing conditions. These sensors will send the information to your phone, tablet, or computer, usually via Bluetooth or Wi-Fi. The app or website that reads the data will typically compare it to a large database of plants to give you specific advice about when to water plants or what conditions to alter (sunlight, temperature, and so on) for optimal growth. The sensors can be designed for indoor plants or outdoor environments, and some function well in both. To start, check out the SEEKONE 4 in 1 Soil Tester ($27.99, Amazon.com), or Scotts Gro Water Sensor Kit ($99.99, Mygro.com).

- **Click & Grow Smart Garden Indoor Gardening Kit** ($79.95, ClickandGrow.com). The Click and Grow Smart Garden is great for growing culinary herbs (basil, mint, and so on) indoors all year long. There are pre-seeded plant capsules you can order, and set up is as simple as dropping the plant capsule into the container, refilling the water reservoir, and plugging in the device. This system is a nice way to garden before you take on larger outdoor projects.

- **Parrot Pot Smart Connected Flower Pot** ($54.99, Amazon .com). The Parrot Pot comes with an automatic watering system that helps keep your plants alive and thriving anywhere in your home. It is a great tool for those who often forget about their plants because this smart pot knows exactly how much water to give to your flora and when. It is available in white, black, and brick. Inside the Parrot Pot are four sensors to accurately assess and process the temperature, sunlight, fertilizer level, and even soil moisture.

GET A FITBIT

You have your choice of many activity monitors with lots of different features, from several manufacturers. In terms of style, we like Apple's watch the best. In terms of value and features, however, we opt for the Fitbit. Fitbit has been around for quite a while and produces well-built hardware, with a useful collection of features and an excellent and easy to use interface to an app that works on iOS and Android devices. You can sync the Fitbit to an iOS or Android device or directly to your computer. Either way, you need a cloud account that will store your data and give you the ability to track your progress.

Fitbit has several models. The one we like the best and think works the best for most people, the Charge 2, lists for $149, but we have recently seen it available in Costco for less.

The Charge 2 comes with a removable band you can replace with a variety of bands available from Fitbit or for a lot less from third parties easily located on Amazon.com.

The Charge 2 easily and automatically records your steps and physical activity, the number of floors you climb in a day, the number of calories you burn (estimated), and how well and how long you sleep (it records and analyzes the time sleeping, allocating it to deep sleep, REM sleep, and light sleep stages). Oh yeah, we almost forgot, it also functions as a watch, keeping track of the time. The Charge 2 has a relatively long battery life (about four to five days when fully charged). Accordingly, you can wear it both day and night to track activities and sleep. You can even get information about calls and messages from your smartphone, as long as you have it relatively nearby (within Bluetooth range). The Charge 2 does not have its own Global Positioning System (GPS), but if you connect it to a GPS-enabled smartphone, the Charge 2 can take advantage of the phone's GPS.

Fitbit has recently announced the impending release of the updated Charge 3. The Charge 3 will replace the 2 in Fitbit's lineup, providing an improved version of the 2. The Charge 3 will start at the same $149.95 price point as its predecessor. (Expect price discounts on the Charge 2 as retailers endeavor to get rid of existing merchandise.) The Charge 3 looks very similar to the Charge 2 but offers a slimmer waterproof design, limited app support, and somewhat longer battery life per charge (up to seven days vs. up to five days). Fitbit has also announced a special edition Charge 3 for $169.95 that also comes with Fitbit Pay, which will enable you to use the device to pay for certain things.

LASER POINTERS CAN MAKE GREAT PET TOYS

Whether or not you consider your pet a hobby, playing with pets often brings the same benefits as engaging in a hobby (and then some). If you have a dog or a cat as a pet, consider spending a few dollars for a red laser pointer. The pointer will help you get your pet some exercise without putting as much strain on you as trying to keep up otherwise. You can find the pointers at many pet stores or online.

Once you get the pointer, stand behind the pet and point it ahead of him or her, to protect against the pet looking directly at the laser point. Aim it at the wall or floor in front of the pet. Bounce the point around, as motion attracts animals' interest. Most dogs and cats will find the point irresistible and try to catch it. As they do, you move it from one place to another. Your pet can get more exercise this way without wearing you out. In fact, you can just stand or sit and use the laser to play with your pet for as long as you like or until the pet tires of it that day.

If you get a laser pointer, be careful with it as they can cause damage to eyes. Do not point it so that your pet can look directly at it (and be sure that you do not point it so that anyone can look directly into the pointer, including yourself). Note that the pointer works best indoors or in a shaded area, but some will work acceptably in open space, even on a fairly bright day.

While lasers come in many colors, we have only seen pointers available for consumers with red or green lasers. While we like the green lasers better for presentations, we prefer the red ones for this use, as the green lasers have more power, so we consider them potentially more risky if the pet turns suddenly and you are not paying attention. With respect to the risk associated with laser pointers, we found the following information on ScientificAmerican.com:

> Eye damage from a pocket laser is unlikely but could be possible under certain conditions. Red laser pointers that are "properly labeled" in the 3–5 mW range have not caused eye damage—no retinal damage has been reported—but there are very real concerns. One is pointers not manufactured to federal specifications. There are reports that green lasers, improperly imported to the U.S., far exceed safety limits.
>
> The Food and Drug Administration's Center for Devices and Radiological Health (FDA) is responsible for light products, including lasers. The FDA regulates the devices and how they are classified and labeled. A class 2 is "safer" than a class 3. Many laser pointers are in the range of 1 to 5 milliwatts (mW), a subclass of 3 called 3A. A close reading of exposure limits indicate that a 5 mW laser could cause eye damage.[3]

---

3. *Can a Pocket Laser Damage the Eye?*, SCIENTIFIC AMERICAN, https://www.scientificamerican.com/article/can-a-pocket-laser-damage/ (last accessed July 19, 2018).

KEEP TRACK OF YOUR PETS WITH LINKAKC

We love our pets; they evolve into members of the family. None of us wants to go through the heartbreak of losing a pet, particularly when the pet just wanders off one day. We want to locate and recover our pets. We even stick microchips under their skin to help people figure out to whom they belong if they run away; but not everyone who finds our pet may know about the microchip or have a microchip reader. There must be more that we can do in this age of technology. Sure enough, technology has come up with another solution to help you find a missing pet: the smart collar! Yes, they even have smart collars for your dog. The Link takes advantage of Bluetooth and cellular technology (it works using AT&T as a provider) to keep track of your pet and your pet's activities throughout the United States (limited to an available AT&T connection).

You put the device into the collar and put the collar on your pet. You keep track of your dog through a smartphone app available for iOS and Android phones. The Link can keep track of your pet's location and will notify you if the dog leaves a "safe zone" that you establish with the app. The Link even has a light that you can control by remote to provide added safety for your pet at night and to make the animal more visible when you try to find it and it is hiding at night. It also has a remote sound capability to help you with training your dog.

In addition to keeping track of your pet's location, the device also tracks your pet's activity levels and will make recommendations for activity levels predicated on the dog's breed. For those of you who leave your dog in the car occasionally, the device will also warn you if the dog is in an environment that has grown too hot or too cold for its health.

The trackers come with a variety of sized collars to fit almost every breed. The collars fit neck sizes from nine to 25 inches.

All in all, we like the Link a lot. It is not perfect; the battery life is one of the biggest issues. Like with your smartphone, you have to remember to recharge the Link. The company advertises the battery as lasting up to two days (we think you should recharge it every night as two days is more wishful thinking than reality). They also claim water resistance to three feet (we have not tested that claim) and impact resistance. The Link lists for $149, but has recently been on sale for $75, $99, and $129. Do note that if you get one of these devices, you also need to subscribe to a connection service to use it. The subscription will cost you $9.95/month per unit, if you want a monthly bill. You can get a discount to $7.95/month per unit by paying for a year in advance and to $6.95/month per unit by paying for two years in advance. We think it makes a great deal of sense to have one of these on your dog if you take the dog outside of your house with you. It also makes sense to use the light if you walk your dog at night, as an extra safety feature for the dog.

It comes with a leather buckle collar. You can also get a separate sports sleeve to hold the tracker. The sports sleeve has a snap collar rather than a buckle collar. You may want to get one of those ($24) as a safety feature for when you take the dog out of the house and plan to encounter other dogs (such as at the dog park). When dogs play they sometimes grab at each other's neck area and can get caught in each other's collars. In that event, the buckle collar poses a hazard and an inconvenience, as you have to pull it tighter to get it to release. That can sometimes prove much harder than releasing a snap collar, particularly as dogs tend to pull when tangled together. Some dogs have strangled in that situation. The snap collar reduces the likelihood of that happening.

The Link is designed for dogs, but if your cat fits the collar, you can get one and use it to keep track of your cat's location (the other features will not work with the cat). You can discover more about the Link and order one online at LinkAKC.com (and yes, if you were wondering, the AKC does stand for the American Kennel Club).

GET FITBARK FOR YOUR DOG

If you do not need to have GPS tracking for your dog and you want to track the dog's activities and save a few dollars, choose FitBark 2. FitBark 2 will monitor Rover's activities and sleep, tracking distance traveled, activity level, calories burned, and time sleeping. The FitBark 2 is relatively small and simply attaches to the dog's collar. In a fit of design cleverness, the FitBark 2 looks like a small bone. FitBark 2 only comes in one model and costs $69.95. One of the best things about FitBark 2 is that its battery life is projected at up to six months. It works on land and in the water, so your dog can wear it for pretty much whatever activities it gets into doing. You can get covers for the device in many covers (see FitBark.com to explore all the color options).

Not surprisingly, the FitBark 2 has an app to allow you to sync and review the data from the device.

The device monitors the general health of your dog to help you know if you need to think about taking the dog to the vet. Interestingly, the FitBark can link to your Fitbit, Apple Watch, Healthkit, or Google Fit device to monitor your workout and your dog's together. Check it out at https://www.fitbark.com.

BECOME A SEASONED PHOTOGRAPHER

Photography offers a lot of benefits as a hobby for seniors. It demands concentration, attention to details, and learning new techniques. It offers the opportunity to express yourself and your view of the world around you. It has been shown to help with overcoming psychological and even physical struggles. Learning photography can improve memory, keeping your mind not only busy, but challenged with something that may be unfamiliar to you.

Photography requires memorizing camera options, focus, and attention to details. For your photos to turn out the way you want them to, you need to take into account composition (the placement or arrangement of visual elements) as well as visual balance. Photography also encourages creativity and problem-solving skills, healthy mental exercise for you to undergo. Getting out of your comfort zone and being creative stimulates your brain to grow new neurons, and stimulates communication between various parts of your brain.

Photography can boost your self-esteem, especially as your skill improves. It provides a sense of accomplishment. This art you create is personal and sharing it with others can increase your dopamine levels, the neurotransmitter chemical that gives you that "good feeling." It is similar to the dopamine effect people experience while exercising. Dopamine helps your mind focus and concentrate, protecting your brain from aging and warding off depression.

If you are interested in taking this up as a hobby, here are some of the tools you will need:

- **Camera**. If you already own a digital camera, start with that. If you intend to go out and buy one, you might check out the Nikon D7000 or D7100. Both are good starter cameras and you can often find discounts when you buy them online. For the Nikon D7000, there is a camera bundle on Amazon .com ($1,050) that includes the camera, lens, bag, and several other accessories to make getting started easier. As you gain experience, you can upgrade lenses and flash to accommodate your needs.

- **Lenses**. Lenses are what help you get the light to the sensor in the camera. Many system cameras will come with one or two lenses as part of the starting package, but additional lenses can range from reasonable to unbelievably expensive. Start out slow; we do not recommend buying up extra lenses until you know what you want or need. If you use a Nikon camera like the one recommended earlier, a good first lens purchase would be the Nikon 35mm f/1.8G AF-S DX AF NIKKOR ($197, Amazon.com).

- **Tripod**. This simple device is often undervalued, but it is actually very important. You might feel inclined to go cheap here, but a quality tripod will serve you much better starting out, especially if your hands are not as steady as they once were. If you go to purchase one, check out the Manfrotto MT190X3 ($152, Amazon.com).

- **Software**. Once you capture the image, you will need the tools to process it. We highly recommend Adobe Photoshop Lightroom ($119.98, Adobe.com). Adobe also offers their photo software as a web-based cloud service for $9.99/month, which will include up to one terabyte of cloud storage.

- **Lighting**. This is especially important if you plan to take a lot of photos with people as your subject. You may want to deviate away from name brand flashes to save some money here, as you can get the same quality images without the cost (Nikon flashes tend to cost hundreds of dollars). If you are looking for lighting, check out the Yongnuo Professional Flash YN 560 III ($63, Amazon.com).

BUILD YOUR OWN VIDEO-RECORDING STUDIO FROM YOUR iPAD WITH PADCASTER

If you enjoy making videos, you can easily incorporate this into your social media marketing with a few tools. The iPad offers enough features that, when combined with the right tools, make it a suitable way to record videos for the web. You can incorporate a video into your practice in a lot of ways. Providing a video on your website is an easy way to give potential clients a sense of how competent and comfortable you are with the area of law you practice without taking up time for a one-on-one interview. It is an opportunity for potential clients to get to know you without leaving the comfort of their home. You can put videos on YouTube, Vimeo, Facebook, and other social media sites as part of your online marketing.

To get started, prop your iPad up with a stand to get it at the angle you prefer, then open the camera app and switch the mode from "Photo" to "Video" in the menu at the bottom right of the screen. Use your finger to slide the menu up or down to get to the video option. If you need to switch from the rear camera to the front, tap the white camera in a shaded circle on the right side of the screen. When you have everything set up, press the red circle button to record. The red circle will turn into a red square, which is the button you will press to stop recording when you are ready to do so. Videos shot this way will get saved in your photos, either organized by date or in a videos folder in your albums. The iOS camera app has both autoexposure and autofocus, which helps when shooting videos yourself.

This is an okay way to start. But you can produce a higher quality video from your iPad, one worthy of your website and social media marketing sites, with the Padcaster Ultimate Studio ($1,299.99, Padcaster.com). The Ultimate Studio is a pre-assembled kit of all the tools you would need to make filming a breeze. You get the Padcaster, a case for your iPad with the tripod mount and the ability to attach additional production equipment to its frame, three microphones (a shotgun mic, a stick mic, and the lavalier mic), a dual mic/ headphone splitter, 0.45x wide angle lens, light-emitting diode (LED) light, 5 feet × 7 feet portable green screen with carry case, Padcaster mini-teleprompter, and the backpack to store all the gear. The Ultimate Studio is great if you are not sure what you will need but you want it all to be there. If you know what you will need and use, you can build a custom studio including only those things. For instance, if you do not think you will use three microphones or the teleprompter, you can put together a studio with everything else and come out to around $850, a $450 savings. The Padcaster case by itself is $189.99, with the tripod running around $169.99. You may be able to buy these tools from different providers and save money, but you will likely spend a lot of time getting it all to work together; there is value in a setup designed to work together and get you recording faster.

Once your video is recorded, you can edit it on the iPad with iMovie. This is a decently powerful tool that comes preinstalled on your iPad. It can match the color between two videos if they were recorded at different times with different lighting. You can overlay one video of another for a picture-in-picture effect. It has a stabilization feature if your video is shaky (if you were holding the iPad while recording for instance).

With these tools you can have an in-office or in-house production studio set up in no time. If you enjoy doing it, you can even continue the process, making and publishing your own podcasts.

MAKE BACK THE COST OF THIS BOOK IN A COUPLE OF WEEKS BY WATCHING MOVIES

If you enjoy spending some time at the local cinema, have we got a tip for you! Recently, a service called MoviePass came out offering the ability to see current movies at the local theater for a fraction of the normal price of admission!

MoviePass sells subscriptions to movies for less than $10 per person per month. Go to their website, https://www.movie pass.com, and sign up for a subscription. They send you a MoviePass Mastercard. Take the Mastercard with you when you go to a movie at a participating theater. The card only works for the movies, but it gets you into three movies a month. (Note that the number used to be much higher but was cut back for financial reasons.) With movies costing more than $9 on average (at least where we live), if you go to the movies three times a month, you will save more than the cost of this book in less than two months. Given the cost of movies, if you use MoviePass once a month you more or less break even, but if you go at least twice a month, you save using MoviePass. You can cancel your MoviePass subscription at any time.

MoviePass operates with some fairly simple rules:

1. You must sign in to the MoviePass app (available for iOS and Android devices) and reserve the movie you want to see.
2. You can only sign in when you are within 100 yards of the theater you plan to visit.
3. You can only see movies in standard format. If you want 3D or IMAX, you cannot use MoviePass and you have to buy a regular ticket for the show.
4. After you sign in, go to the ticket window and ask for a ticket to the show.
5. Give them your MoviePass card and they will run it like a credit card. If you have done Steps 1–4 properly,

the charge will go through and the cashier will hand you your ticket.

6. You will not receive a bill for charging any movie tickets. You will only receive a bill for the monthly subscription (which MoviePass charges to another credit card you set up when you subscribe).

7. You can only get one ticket per subscription, so you will need a second subscription for your spouse or functional equivalent if you want a MoviePass ticket for that person.

8. Once you sign up for a particular movie, you cannot sign up for another one the same day, unless you first cancel the original movie. You cannot cancel after you get a ticket. If you get to the ticket window and learn that they have sold out the showing you planned to see, you can cancel the reservation and replace it with a later showing of the same film that day or another movie entirely.

MoviePass does not work in every theater, as some do not allow the use of the service. It works in a lot of theaters, however. We have used it in several cities and have had no problem locating participating theaters in U.S. cities we have visited. From our observations, it appears to work in most theaters (at least in the areas we have visited).

In the face of the MoviePass model, some theater chains have started their own programs. For example, AMC has modified its loyalty program by adding what it calls "A-List" as an option. To join A-List, you have to belong to the AMC Stubbs program (free to join) and pay $19.95 plus tax each month for the A-List privileges. A-List lets you see three movies a week but only at AMC theaters. A-List works much more simply than MoviePass. When you sign up for A-List (which you do through the AMC app you download to your smartphone) you get a payment card that lives in your smartphone (in your Apple Wallet if you have an iPhone). With A-List, you go to the ticket window and order the tickets you want. You show them the payment card in your smartphone and they scan a code there, which the system accepts as payment. They give you the ticket and you go see your movie. That's all there is to it.

Unlike MoviePass, you can also reserve your tickets in advance using the AMC app. Unlike MoviePass, the AMC program includes upgrades from standard movies (such as IMAX movies).

If your regular theater is part of the AMC organization, the AMC Stubs A-List may be a better choice for you. If you see a lot of movies at AMC and elsewhere, you might even consider both, as you will pay only $30 per month for both and could see as many as 15 movies in a month using the two cards.

BECOME THE FAMILY ARCHIVER

Do you have an interest in preserving your family photos? Over a lifetime you may find you have accumulated boxes upon boxes of photos that rarely see the light of day, let alone have the opportunity to be oooh'd and aaaah'd over like they should. We touched on doing something with family photos earlier, but many will find working with family photos to be an enjoyable hobby.

The digital era comes with an unimaginable number of tools to preserve your treasured memories. Preserving your memories electronically not only frees up the physical space around you, it also organizes the memories in a meaningful way that makes them even more accessible. This helps ensure they can be passed on to the next generation.

Your first step to archive family photos is to digitize your analog photos and keepsakes. If you have a smartphone, the fastest and easiest way to do this is by using your phone's built-in camera to snap a photo of the picture that you can then upload to your computer. You can also use a scanner if you have the hardware. A flatbed scanner would likely work best, depending on the size of the photo or document. Automatic feed scanners are not suitable for fragile, weak, or valuable papers. You should not just limit it to photos either. Capture images of marriage records, birth records, family bibles, and your children's old school projects. Digitizing these records allows you to view and share the items without the risk of damage by handling.

Do not feel daunted by photo slides or negatives. You can find a service that can process these. Some services allow you to ship boxes to them for preservation, while others will drive to your home and digitize everything for you there. You might feel more comfortable with a home service, depending on the content of the slides or negatives.

As you accumulate more digital files, how you name and organize the files will become more important. When naming your files, feel free to use any alphanumeric combination that makes sense to you, but avoid using spaces, punctuation marks, or symbols. Try using hyphens or underscores instead of spaces. While naming your files, it is a good idea to add basic metadata to the file if you can, such as the date the picture was taken, who was in it, what was happening then, and so on. Adding metadata is akin to writing on the back of a photograph.

Digital cameras and smartphones will capture and apply some metadata automatically, such as the date the photo was taken, file size, and type. If you capture a photo with a smartphone it can even include the location of the photo (if you have that feature enabled).

There are many ways to add metadata yourself, including software such as Adobe Photoshop or Google Photos. Prior to 2016, Picasa was our go-to suggestion for beginner digital archiving, but Google retired the software and no longer offers support for it. Google Photos is a logical next best thing, and has a lot of the same features as Picasa did, though some users found the photo editor in Picasa more robust.

Make sure you keep a backup of your digitized files as you progress. When it comes to preserving the digitized files of your memories, the National Archives recommends you follow the 3-2-1 Rule, which stands for three copies, stored on two different media, and one copy located off-site. The concept was popularized by Peter Krogh, a well-known photographer who wrote that there are two groups of people: those who have already had a storage failure and those who will have one in the future. One easy way to apply this rule is by having your data stored on your computer (copy one), with a regular on-site backup either through your network or removable media storage device (copy two), and in the cloud (copy three). The cloud backup serves the multipurpose of being a third copy, on a different media, and off-site. There are a lot of cloud media storage services out there. A popular one to try (especially if you are an Amazon Prime member) is Amazon's Prime Photos. You can also use Google Photos, the web service suggested earlier.

One of the most enjoyable parts of being the family archiver is sharing the preserved memories with friends and family. There are a number of great ways to share your memories with the people you care about and future generations. You can easily share prints of your photos (whether manually digitized by you or captured with a digital camera or smartphone). There are many services that will send physical photo prints to anyone you want with a few finger taps or mouse clicks. If you use an Android or iOS phone, you may want to check out the Free-Prints app, a print and delivery service that will allow you to print and send a certain number of photos every month for free, and all you pay is shipping. There is no subscription or commitment required, and the more you use it, the more additional freebies you get. The free photo offer will print 4 inch × 6 inch photos with a matte or glossy finish. You can pay to upgrade to a larger size or unlock offers for a free 5 inch × 7 inch photo after a certain number of uses. It is very easy to capture and print photos from social media or any other photo-sharing sites. You simply save or download the photo to your phone, the app connects to your photos, and you tap the ones you want printed. Then tell the app where you want the photos to go and pay for the shipping and you are done. No more driving to stores and waiting for prints. Prime Photos, mentioned earlier, will also print and deliver photos for you. They will charge $0.09/print for a 4 inch × 6 inch photo, but the shipping is free for Amazon Prime subscribers, which makes the cost about the same as the FreePrints app.

Another way of sharing the memories is through photo books, which can be easily created through many of the print websites. If you have taken a once-in-a-lifetime trip, a photo book makes a great keepsake. If you have digitized your parents' and grandparents' photos and records, compiling them into a book with captions and sharing some of the stories behind the documents and images is a great way to preserve and share your history. It tells the story long after you are gone, and can easily be stored on bookshelves and passed down to the next generation.

Keep in mind this oft-quoted concept: when an old person dies, it is as if a library is burned down. It is easy, and usually pretty fun, to preserve your history, your library, for future generations.

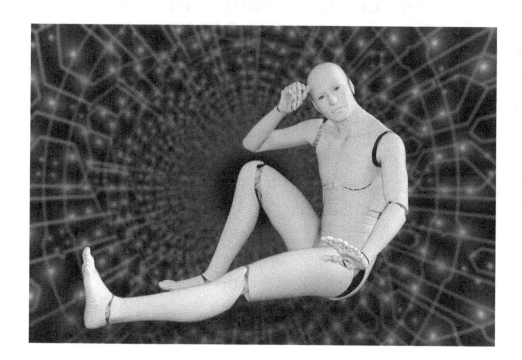

MISCELLANEOUS TECHNOLOGY TIPS

INCLUDE INSTRUCTIONS FOR DIGITAL RECORDS IN YOUR SUCCESSION PLAN AND YOUR EMERGENCY PLAN

No one knows when a medical disaster will strike, but we know that they do. We should all have plans in place for such unforeseen events. Regarding your practice, you have an ethical obligation to have a plan in place for such contingencies. In both your personal and professional lives, you need to consider technology in developing such plans.

If you work in a multi-lawyer firm, it may prove easier for you to make such plans professionally. If you are a solo practitioner, then you especially need to heed this advice and it is a more difficult prospect to complete. If you do not have a plan in place already, put one together now. Do not wait for your work to slow down, because your health will not wait for you. Sadly, this tip is hitting close to home for one of the authors (Ashley). She has a family member with a solo estate planning practice in Texas, whose support staff consisted of his wife and daughter. At a family holiday gathering, the topic of busy workloads and no time for vacations came up. She asked him if he had a legacy plan in place—what would happen if he were hit by a bus? He dismissed the idea and the holiday merriment ensued. Three months later, he suffered a massive stroke during a hearing at court. He had no plan in place.

The time to plan for a medical setback is now. If your medical disaster results in a temporary disability, digital records can make it easier for your designated caretaker attorney to look after your clients while you are recovering. However, having digital records is not enough. There are steps you need to take to make these records available and useful.

The first step is to designate a caretaker attorney, and make sure office staff, and family members, know who the attorney is and how to contact the attorney. For the designated attorney, make sure he or she knows:

1. How and where you maintain your calendar

2. Contact information for all current staff
3. The names and passwords to all computers
4. Any other office procedures for calendaring, collecting and opening mail, and filing
5. Where files are located and where you store archived files
6. Usernames and passwords for all accounts used in your practice

For your digital files, put together a memorandum or manual explaining:

1. Are your computers networked?
2. Who has access to which parts of the network?
3. How are client files organized on the computer?
4. What backup procedures do you use?
5. Is a digital calendar maintained on the computer?
6. Is billing kept on the computer?
7. For e-mail, document the program used, username, and password.

Maintaining a digital record of your business accounts for services, including websites, usernames, and passwords, can go a long way to helping staff and the caretaker attorney maintain your practice and protect your clients during recovery. It will also assist staff and family members if you are permanently incapacitated.

You should also maintain similar information for your personal accounts to assist your family in the event of your death or disability.

SAVE MONEY BY BUYING NEW OLDER TECHNOLOGY

The folks who manufacture smartphones have made a great deal of money by convincing us that we need to get a new smartphone every year or two. Many people have followed that same philosophy when it comes to tablets as well. We are here to tell you "it ain't necessarily so." For example, Apple built the iPhone 7 and 7 Plus. These phones registered at the top of the scale in terms of sophistication, style, convenience, and utility when they first came out. Similarly, Samsung released its Galaxy 8 series, also at the top of the scale.

Then, Samsung released the Galaxy S9 series and Apple released both the iPhone 8 and the iPhone X and now the XS and XS Max. Make no mistake about it, the Galaxy S9 bests the S8 and the iPhone 8 bests the iPhone 7, while the iPhone X bests the iPhone 8, and the iPhone XS improves on the iPhone X. Interestingly, many people have purchased the iPhone 8, even though the X offers more, simply because it cost less and was "good enough." Even more interestingly, the iPhone 7 still works well. It offers exactly the same sophistication, style, and power as it did the year before. More interesting still, Apple continues to show the iPhone 7 and iPhone 7 Plus as current technology, but because it came out a year earlier than the 8 and X, Apple has made a significant adjustment in the price. You can get a brand new iPhone 7 for less than it cost when it came out and also less than the 8. You can no longer order a new iPhone X from Apple (though you may be able to get it from third parties). The XS and XS Max have replaced it. Do you need the additional advances of the 8 or the XS? More likely than not, you do not, and the 7 would work just as well for you.

You will find the same analysis applies to almost all electronic devices, not just smartphones. We have seen it in relation to tablets, laptop computers, desktop computers, smartwatches, digital cameras, and on and on. Recognize, however, that while such things as digital cameras may continue to work well indefinitely, smartphones do ultimately become obsolete. As time goes on and new operating systems come out, last year's phone may work fine with the new system, but the one you got five or six years ago may no longer work as well. Operating systems and software ultimately evolve to take advantage of newer processors and additional memory or other technology included in a newer device. The bottom line is that much of the technology will work for several years, but, ultimately, it will stop working well and you will need to replace it at that time (if not sooner). That means that if you buy older technology, it may not last as long as the brand new technology that replaced it.

SAVE MONEY BY BUYING TOP-OF-THE-LINE TECHNOLOGY AND HOLDING ON TO IT LONGER

This tip goes in the opposite direction of the last one. Not because one works better than the other, but because it reflects a different perspective and perception of how to handle technology.

It shares with the last tip the belief that technology has a longer life span than the manufacturers and vendors want you to believe, but it recognizes that a piece of technology, such as a smartphone, has a finite life and will, ultimately, require replacement. As a general rule, if you get the latest and greatest device, it will still work a year or two longer than the year-or-two-old version you bought new at the same time. Accordingly, if you want to keep it for five or six years as opposed to three or four years, you may find that it works better to get the top of the line, knowing you will pay more for it when you get it, but that you will hold on to it for a couple more years (as opposed to paying less for the older technology and replacing it sooner).

One way you get the fun of the top end of the line for a couple of years but pay a premium price when you buy it; the other way you buy more often but spend less each time. Which will save you the most money over a ten-year period? That depends on how often you update your technology. If you follow the guidelines below, you will likely buy two new smartphones over the ten-year period. If you follow the advice in the previous tip, you will likely buy three new smartphones over the same ten-year period but pay reduced prices for each of them. Both of these approaches work and make considerable sense. Which one you follow depends on your personal prefer-ences. Either way you will likely spend about the same on the technology over a ten-year period. The one way you will spend con-siderably more for technology is to follow the urgings of the vendors and replace your technology more frequently (like every year or two for your smartphone).

To make your decision a bit easier, here are some guidelines that we find work fairly well if you buy top-end technology each time you buy. You will likely find some variation from time to time, such as when the cell phone providers ultimately switch from 4G to the much faster and more powerful 5G technology, currently on the horizon. When that happens, you may want to replace your phone sooner to take advantage of the newer technology; conversely, you will not have to, as they will not simply shut down the 4G technology (we still have 3G technology in general use, even though we have had 4G phones for many years; we will probably have 5G technology in general use long before we have universal 4G coverage in place).

Note that regarding the following table, the care you take of the device, the amount you use it, and the quality you purchased originally will all bear on the useful life of the device. For those making limited use of their devices, you may find that some of them, particularly computers and cameras, will still work fine even after the range suggested below. We know of some people using equipment many years older than the outside ranges we recommend. While your devices may continue to function, after a while you end up depriving yourself of many excellent features and advances. For that reason, we recommend replacement of the devices on a fairly regular basis. We have stayed on the shorter side of the list below in almost all cases and often replaced equipment sooner than the short side of the schedule. We have also saved some of our older technology and gone back after several years to see how it worked in comparison to the newer technology. Sometimes the performance pleasantly surprised us, but most of the time we found the older hardware slower and noticeably less capable.

Device	Estimated Useful Life
Desktop computer	4–6 years
Laptop computer	4–5 years
Tablet	3–5 years
Smartphone	3–5 years
Digital camera	6–8 years
Video camera	5–7 years

I CAN HEAR YOU NOW!

These days you can hardly walk down the street without seeing several people with any variety of earphone devices sticking out of, riding on, or surrounding their ears. Sometimes those devices work simply as earphones or headsets to allow the wearer to listen to recorded audio information (podcasts, lectures, music, and so on). Sometimes they function as connections to cell phones. Sometimes they do double duty and handle both functions.

Many of us have experienced some loss of hearing acuity by the time we reach adulthood and more as we age. Hearing aid technology has come a long way and many manufacturers have come up with invisible (or at least very hard to see) models of such devices. Some even come with Bluetooth technology so they can also function as telephone headsets.

Unfortunately, most of the hearing aid devices look like hearing aids and not like the headsets or earphones you see so often on the streets. If you have longish hair or get one of the virtually invisible models of the hearing aid, it may make no difference. If you have short hair, have grown follicularly challenged, or get a larger and more visible hearing aid, you may be disinclined to wear it as often as you should. For reasons we have never quite figured out, people seem more willing to acknowledge that their eyes need help than their ears do. Most people who need help seeing get it, but many who need help hearing do not, and, therefore, just get by. We suspect that results from embarrassment or expense, as hearing aids can prove quite costly.

The folks at Bose came up with a clever idea designed to help those with moderate hearing loss. In 2017, Bose (https://www.bose.com) brought out its conversation-enhancing "Hearphones." The Hearphones, which look like many other Bluetooth earphones designed to function as both standard headsets for recorded audio playback and as telephone headsets, also work to enhance normal conversation, making it easier to hear people you are talking to in a crowded or noisy environment (like those sitting at your table in a restaurant). Just out of curiosity, did you ever wonder why they seem to always design restaurants to capture and recirculate the noise making it very hard to carry on a conversation in a busy restaurant? The Hearphones can help solve that problem. The Hearphones are a hearing assistance device, they are not hearing aids. They do not qualify as medical devices and do not require a doctor's prescription. That also means that your medical insurance will not cover them, even if it covers hearing aids. You can find more information about the Hearphones on the Bose website or by visiting a Bose retail store or outlet.

Bose also released an app available for both iOS and Android devices that gives you better control over the functionality of the Hearphones than the buttons on the Hearphones.

The Hearphones have Bose's active noise cancellation technology (Bose has long been recognized as one of the best, if not the best, producers of such technology). The Hearphones come with a nice carrying case, charge in about three hours with Universal Serial Bus (USB) or near-field communication (NFC) charging technology, and work for nine to ten hours off of a full charge.

If you have problems hearing conversation in crowded or noisy environments, check these out at the local Bose store. They may prove just the ticket. While they do not come cheaply (nothing with the Bose name does), the $499 price tag represents a fraction of the cost of most hearing aids. In case you were wondering, they also do a very good job with audio playback and work with iOS 10 or later and Android 4.4 "KitKat" or later.

USE YOUR SMARTPHONE AS A MAGNIFIER

Back in the day, many people carried a small magnifying glass in their pocket or purse and also kept one in or on their desk. Even if you have good vision, sometimes the print on something you have to read is so small you find it hard to read. Some of us struggle to read the really small print even with glasses. Thanks to the wonders of modern technology, you no longer need that magnifying glass. You just need to pull out your trusty smartphone and use one of its many hidden talents.

If you take a picture of a label with the camera in your smartphone, you can view the picture and open it up large enough that whatever you had to read becomes easily readable. With most modern smartphones you do not even need to take the picture, as you can expand the image in the display prior to snapping the photo and read it from the expanded image without ever taking the picture. On the other hand, if you are looking at something you may need to refer to again for whatever reason, push the shutter button and then flag the image so you can more easily find it later, saving yourself the trouble of going through the process again. Another good reason to not leave home without your smartphone!

Hint: With most contemporary smartphones, you expand the image of the photo or the pre-photo display by placing your thumb and forefinger together on the display at the point you want to read and slowly moving them apart from each other while maintaining contact with the display.

USE FOLDERS TO SORT YOUR APPLICATIONS

While this tip may seem so basic that some of you wonder why we included it, it continues to surprise us how often we look at someone else's smartphone or tablet and see apps strewn all over the place and in no particular order. Yes, you can always locate the app using the search features built into the iOS or Android operating systems, but that normally requires you to remember the name of the application, or at least some part of it. If you cannot remember enough of the name for the search facility to locate the app, you can either forget about using it or you can look through your applications, one by one, page by page, until you find it. We can guarantee that if and when you do find it, you will do so at the very end of your quest to do so; it will always be the last app you see in the search.

We have found it very helpful to organize applications on smartphones and tablets into folders. Both the iOS and the Android systems allow you to do that (although we find doing so with iOS a bit easier). If you divide your applications into subjects, label the folders by the subject, and then put the apps into the folders based on that grouping, you will have much better luck locating the app you want, especially if you cannot remember its name.

Folder titles we have used include:

Augmented Reality	News
Auto	Newspapers/
Books	Magazines
Business	Notes/Outlines
Calculators	Presentations
Documents	Productivity
Education	Reference
Entertainment	Scan/Fax/Print
Financial	Signature
Games	Sports
Graphics	Travel
Health	Utilities
Legal	Videos
Microsoft	Weather
Mind Maps	Wi-Fi
Navigation	

You may find that some of these folder headings fit your needs perfectly, while others do not. We do not suggest them to you as headings you should have, only as examples of headings we have used. Select the groupings/headings that work best for you and your collection of applications. If, for example, you want a particular application for document execution and you cannot think of its name, you will find it much easier if you have all of your document execution applications in a folder labeled for that (we use "Signature"), as you can simply go to that folder and select the app you wanted, even if you forgot its name.

POP, IMAP, AND EXCHANGE . . . OH MY!

If you have set up an e-mail client before, you have likely come across the options POP3, IMAP, and Exchange. These options represent protocols and refer to the method by which the app you are using will access and download your e-mail. To clarify, here is a brief description of each:

POP3. Post Office Protocol (POP) is the oldest and most established protocol. It was created back in 1984, when Internet connections were intermittent, slow, and spotty. It was engineered as a simple way to download copies of your e-mail for offline reading. With the current iteration of POP (POP3), your application connects to an e-mail server and downloads the messages to your device that have not been previously downloaded. By default, the application will then delete all the original e-mails from your server, although you can alter this setting to leave them on the server for a specified period or sometimes indefinitely. Because of the simplistic protocol, things can get jumbled when checking e-mail on multiple devices (like your computer, smartphone, and tablet). For one, sent e-mails get a little squirrely. The e-mail you send from your e-mail client will get stored on that client, on that device. If you send the e-mail from your desktop, you will not find it in your sent folder on your smartphone. Also, deleting the e-mail deletes it only in the e-mail client you are on, it does not delete it from anywhere else it may have been downloaded. The main perk to POP3 is its speed, and this may be the better way to set up an e-mail if you will only check the e-mail on one device.

IMAP. Internet Message Access Protocol (IMAP) followed closely behind POP in 1986. It is better suited for the modern, always-connected world we are in today.

IMAP allows users to use multiple e-mail clients from multiple devices and view their e-mail as though they were viewing it directly on the server. IMAP leaves all messages stored on the server, rather than downloading them to your e-mail client like POP3 does. With IMAP, if you delete an e-mail from your desktop e-mail client, you will not see it when you open your smart-phone. Similarly, if you send an e-mail from your tablet, you can still find it in your sent folder on your desktop e-mail client.

Microsoft Exchange and MAPI. Microsoft began development on its Messaging Application Program Interface (MAPI) shortly after POP and IMAP emerged. It provides a way for e-mail clients and other applications to communicate with Microsoft Exchange Servers. It operates similar to IMAP for syncing messages, contacts, and calendar entries. If you have used Microsoft Outlook, then you have used the MAPI.

The most popular webmail programs will often let you set up your e-mail client as either POP3 or IMAP, depending on your preference. How do you choose? Here is a quick reference guide:

- If you use check your e-mail from a lot of devices, phones, or computers, then either use a webmail service or set up your e-mail clients to use IMAP.
- If you use mostly webmail and want your phone or tablet to sync with your webmail, then use IMAP as well.
- As we mentioned before, if you only check e-mail in one e-mail client on one dedicated machine, you can use POP3 (although we would still recommend IMAP for convenience).
- If you have a huge history of e-mail and you are using an old e-mail provider that offers little drive space, then you may want to use POP3 to keep your server clean and avoid running out of space.
- If you use a company e-mail, and your company uses an Exchange Server, then you will need to use Exchange.

CHOOSING AN E-MAIL CLIENT

E-mail is a convenient means of communication, but you can increase that convenience by getting yours all in one place with an e-mail client. E-mail clients are desktop software programs that allow you to receive, read, compose, and send e-mails from the e-mail address you register with it. E-mail clients differ from webmail (such as Gmail, Hotmail, and so on) because the program exists on your computer, smartphone, or tablet, and many offer features that webmail does not. You may be wondering if you even need an e-mail client, and

the answer is (in typical legal fashion) . . .
maybe. E-mail clients are handy if you:

- Have multiple e-mail addresses
  (perhaps your professional
  e-mail, a personal e-mail, and an
  e-mail used for newsletters and
  registrations)
- Enjoy having access to e-mail
  offline (e.g., if you can see yourself
  drafting e-mails on an airplane,
  to send when you connect to the
  Internet later)
- Prefer to back up your e-mail
  regularly, or have limited storage
  with your e-mail provider
- Like using digital signatures and
  encryption (which, for your professional e-mail, you should be
  using both)
- Enjoy filtering features that allow
  you to auto sort e-mails into a
  folder based on specific keywords

Common examples of e-mail clients are
Microsoft Outlook and Apple Mail, but
there are several options beyond these that
may better suit your taste. Here are a few
you might like to check out:

- **IncrediMail** (http://www.incredi mail.com). IncrediMail has a reputation for being easy to use and fun. It comes packed with stationery and multimedia content, a useful feature if you like to send catchy, creative e-mail messages. You can organize your e-mail into folders, similar to Apple Mail and Microsoft Outlook. The downside to IncrediMail is it lacks learning filters that allow you to set rules for certain messages to auto-populate designated folders. Also, the free version will include ads in your e-mail, which we do not recommend for your professional e-mail address.

- **Windows Mail**. Windows Mail replaced Outlook Express, so if you are familiar with that system you will find Windows Mail to be easy to use. It is reliable with filtering spam and phishing e-mails. It has built in stationery and some nice editing features. Also, Windows Mail will block

remote content and only allows
you to read messages as plain
text e-mails, a feature that keeps
your e-mail and computers more
secure. Some drawbacks to this
client include the inability to integrate RSS (*R*ich *S*ite *S*ummary or
sometimes called *R*eally *S*imple
*S*yndication) news feeds and the
absence of message templates.

- **Spark** (https://sparkmailapp
.com/). Spark is only available to
MacOS users, but in addition to
Mac computers, it is also available
for iOS and the Apple Watch. You
can access multiple IMAP e-mail
accounts (including iCloud Mail,
Gmail, and Outlook.com), but
POP and Exchange ActiveSync
accounts are not supported.

SEND TALK MESSAGES NOT TEXT MESSAGES

Most of us have developed the habit of sending text messages, as they offer a convenient and silent way of communicating. If silence is not critical and you have discovered that your fingers may have grown too slow for your desires in texting or too chunky to easily get the right keys (or you are simply tired of the auto-incorrect program on your iPhone changing what you wanted to say into something that is very different and may not even make sense), we have a tip for you. A few years ago, Apple built talk or voice messaging into its text messaging application. If you have an iPhone, open up a text messaging screen and look at the bottom right corner of your display. See a microphone icon there. (If you do not see one, then your iOS is too old, and you need to update it.) Android users also have the same feature available, but instead of the microphone, they see the image of a sound wave in a circle in the bottom right corner of their display.

Assuming that you see the microphone, touch it and then start to speak. The iPhone will pick up and record your voice, translate the speech to text, and attach the audio file to the text message. Android phones simply record the audio file and transmit it for playing on the receiving end.

LIKE MAGAZINES?
SUBSCRIBE TO TEXTURE

Lots of us still like to read magazines. Subscribing to all the magazines you might find interesting can become quite costly. Moreover, you may want to read some issues and not others, so you may not want to subscribe to them. Buying magazines at the newsstand costs much more than the subscription price and you can usually get an annual subscription for the same price as a few copies at the newsstand. So, what is a reader to do? We have an answer for you. If you have a tablet or smartphone, you can get an app called Texture. Texture comes on both the iOS and Android platforms, so you pretty much have coverage no matter what your preferred technology. You can get it at Apple's iTunes App Store or at the Google Play Store.

By subscribing to Texture for $9.99/ month, you get the right to read more than 200 magazines on your iOS or Android device, whenever you want. Even better, when you travel, you still only carry your device and it gives you access to all

the magazines. Compare that to having to schlep even a dozen magazines with you on a trip, or paying for them in an airport convenience store. You subscribe to it through the app or by accessing https://www.tex ture.com/ online.

If you find a handful of magazines that you like and read a couple issues a month, you have pretty much paid for the cost of the subscription. The app offers magazines in a number of categories, including automotive, business and finance, crafts and hobby, entertainment, fashion and style, food and cooking, health and fitness, home and gardening, kids and parenting, men's lifestyle, news and politics, science and tech, sports and recreation, travel and regional, and women's lifestyle.

The following is a list of SOME of the titles included in the subscription:

AARP the Magazine

Adweek

Afar

Allrecipes

Allure

Architectural Digest

Automobile

Backpacker

Better Homes & Gardens

Bicycling

Bike

Billboard

Birds & Blooms

Bloomberg Businessweek

Bloomberg Markets

Boating

Bon Appétit

Brides

Car and Driver

Châtelaine (English and Français)

Clean Eating

CNET

Coastal Living

Condé Nast Traveler

Consumer Reports

Cooking Light

Cosmopolitan

Country Gardens

Country Living

Cruising World

Cycle World

Diabetic Living

Do-It-Yourself

Domino

Dwell

EatingWell

Ebony

ELLE

ELLE Decor

Entertainment Weekly

Entrepreneur

ESPN The Magazine

Esquire

Essence

Family Circle

Family Handyman

FamilyFun

Fast Company

Field & Stream

Fit Pregnancy and Baby

Flying

Food & Wine

Food Network Magazine

Forbes

Fortune

Garden & Gun

Glamour

Gluten-Free Living

Golf

Golf Digest

Golf Tips

Good Housekeeping

GQ

GQ Style

Harper's Bazaar

Health

HELLO! Canada

HGTV Magazine

History

Hot Rod

House & Home

House Beautiful

i-D Magazine

In Touch Weekly

Inc.

InStyle

Interior Design

Interview

Life & Style Weekly

LOULOU

Maclean's

Macworld

Make:

Marie Claire

Martha Stewart Living

Martha Stewart Weddings

Maxim

Men's Health

Men's Journal

Midwest Living

Modern Farmer

Money

Mother Jones

Motor Trend

Motorcyclist

National Geographic

National Geographic Kids

National Geographic Traveler

National Review

New York Magazine

NewBeauty

Newsweek

O, the Oprah Magazine

OK!

OUT

Outdoor Life

Outdoor Photographer

Outside

Oxygen

Parents

Parents Latina

PC Magazine

PCWorld

People

People en Español

Popular Mechanics

Popular Science

Prevention

Rachael Ray Every Day

Reader's Digest

Real Simple

Redbook

Road & Track

Rolling Stone

Runner's World

Sailing World

Saveur

Seventeen

Shape

Shutterbug

Simple & Delicious

Simple Grace

SKI

Smithsonian

Sound & Vision

Southern Living

Sport Fishing

Sports Illustrated

Sports Illustrated Kids

Sportsnet

STAR

Successful Farming

Sunset

Surfer

Taste of Home

Tennis

Texas Monthly

The Atlantic

The Hollywood Reporter

The Magnolia Journal

The New Yorker	Vogue
The Pioneer Woman	W Magazine
This Old House	Weight Watchers
Time	Wine Enthusiast
Today's Parent	Wired
Town & Country	Woman's Day
Traditional Home	Woman's World
Travel + Leisure	Women's Health
Truck Trend	Wood
Us Weekly	Working Mother
Vanity Fair	Yoga Journal
Variety	

One other good thing: when you first download the app, you get a seven-day free trial to see if you like it before you have to decide whether to subscribe. You can find out more about the app by looking for it in the Apple iTunes App Store or the Google Play Store or by going online to https://www.texture.com/.

CHECK OUT MAGZTER

Magzter approaches the magazine experience a bit differently than Texture, but some of you may find it very appealing. Magzter comes both for the iOS and the Android platforms; you can get it at the Google Play Store or Apple's iTunes App Store.

Magzter boasts that it has made more than 9,500 magazines available in more than 40 categories and over 60 languages.

What is different about Magzter is that not only does it allow you to pick an issue of a magazine and read it, it also will digest issues for you and select articles that fall into an area in which you have a particular interest.

When you log in, you set up a profile and tell the app the types of things that interest you. It will then select magazines in its catalog that relate to the areas of interest you selected. For example, I selected sports and got a large collection of possible magazines including almost every imaginable sport and both well-known magazines, such as *Sports Illustrated*, and lesser known magazines, such as individual sports team's magazines for many teams and sports. The coverage ranged from basketball to snowboarding and everything in between.

One thing that sets Magzter aside is its ability to curate articles and give you premium articles in specific subject matters. For example, I selected "Apple" (as in the company) and it gave me a choice of 49 articles very relevant to Apple, its direction, its products, and its future.

Magzter comes on a subscription basis. You get a 30-day free trial and then it costs $9.99/month or you can discount it by buying a year subscription for $99.

KEEP TRACK OF YOUR STUFF

While we try to not misplace our possessions, the simple fact is that, occasionally, we all do. Most of us find it frustrating when that happens, particularly when it happens fairly regularly. Unfortunately, many of us find that as we get older, it happens more often. Sometimes misplacing something results from simple forgetfulness. Other times, it results from someone helping himself or herself to our property. Paying attention to not leaving property unattended in public places can help with the latter, but that does little for the former.

The wonders of modern technology can make things easier for you regarding the former. Several manufacturers have come out with devices that you can place in your wallet, purse, briefcase, computer case, iPad case, on your key ring, and so on, that will help you locate them when you forgot where you put them.

We like the TrackR device, as it comes at a fairly reasonable price and has a slim profile that lets you insert it into things such as wallets without taking up too much space or seriously deforming the shape of the wallet. You can even stick it to the case of a smartphone, tablet, or e-reader using double-sided tape.

The TrackR comes in two models. The Pixel model, which costs $24.99 for one and offers significant quantity discounts (an eight-pack costs $99.99), weighs 0.14 ounce and has a profile similar to a coin: round, 1 inch × 1 inch × 0.2 inch. The Bravo model costs $29.99 for one and an eight-pack will run you $149.99. The Bravo has a brushed aluminum cover, weighs in at

0.25 ounce, and measures only 0.14 inch thick. Both models have the same features and come with a light and also a reasonably loud ringer so you can use the sound to help you locate the device to which you attached it (note that you have to be in fairly close proximity to the device to hear it). Both have user-replaceable batteries. The Bravo uses CR160 button batteries. The Pixel uses CR2016 batteries.

The TrackR has both an iOS and an Android app that interface with the device using Bluetooth. If you leave the app running in the background, it will record the last known location of each device, even when you have moved out of Bluetooth range for the device. All the TrackR devices provide an interesting feature: if you press the device, it makes the phone to which you paired it ring, even if you have the phone on silent mode. The TrackR also can get you assistance from other users if you misplace something, as if you have put it into search mode; you will get a notification if the item to which you attached the

TrackR comes within the range of Bluetooth of another tracker user.

You can find out more information and order TrackR devices online at https://secure.thetrackr.com.

WHAT THE []*&^_[%]^ DO I DO WHEN MY COMPUTER FREEZES?

At one time or another, most of us experience the frustration of a computer that just freezes and will do nothing. If and when you find yourself in that situation, the following steps may help you solve the problem:

1. **Restart the computer**. Sometimes simply restarting it will solve the problem. That has proven true often and presents the quickest and easiest step to take.

2. **Shut down the computer**. If a simple restart does not work, sometimes you will have better luck by turning the computer off completely. If you have a desktop, turn it off and then pull the plug, wait about 30 seconds, and plug it in again before restarting the computer. If you have a laptop with a removable battery, remove the battery, wait about 30 seconds, and then reinsert it before you restart the computer. Almost every computer goes through a series of procedures and checks on shutdown and/or start-up that might identify and solve the problem.

3. **Boot up in "safe mode."** If shutting down the computer and then starting it again does not work, try shutting down and booting into "safe mode." In safe mode, the computer ignores a lot of pieces added by collateral programs that might interfere with your start-up process or your operations. It also runs tests and fixes some problems while starting. As a result, booting into safe mode will take

more time than a standard start-up of the computer. To boot into safe mode on the current iterations of the MacOS and Windows, you simply hold the "shift" key down while you restart the computer. Wait until you see the display show that the process is engaged before releasing it (when you see something on the display other than a blank screen you can release it). You will ultimately see an indication that you booted into safe mode. If everything works in safe mode, then the computer repaired itself booting into safe mode. If the problem returns, it is likely that: (1) one of the programs you added to the computer has interfered with its operation; or (2) you have picked up some malware that has interfered with the operations; or (3) you have a hardware failure.

4. **Get some help**. At this point, if you have a fair amount of technological sophistication and the right software, you can run some tests on the computer to see if it has a

hardware failure or has suffered a malware invasion. Some software can identify and isolate (quarantine) the malware and fix the computer. If you do not have the software or the sophistication, you should call Apple Tech Support if you have a Mac, or Microsoft Tech Support if you have a machine running on Windows. Both have phone support, and both offer support on a space available or appointment basis at their retail stores. We recommend making the phone call first and having the technician hold your hand through a series of tests and potential troubleshooting fixes that they can do over the phone before you take the time to go to the retail store.

BE WARY OF PHISHING E-MAIL SCAMS

Phishing e-mail messages are designed to steal money. Cybercriminals that access your computer can install malicious software on it or steal your personal information off it. The e-mails are deceptive, and they often appear to come from familiar enterprises (e.g., your credit card company, your Internet service provider, your bank). The message will usually contain a link that will take you to a spoofed website or otherwise get you to provide your private information.

One common type of phishing attempt is an e-mail message stating that you are receiving it due to fraudulent activity on your account. It will typically ask you to click the link in the e-mail to "verify your information." These scams want to trick you into responding or clicking immediately. They will claim that you will lose something (e.g., access to e-mail or your bank account). This claim should tell you immediately that this is a phishing scam; responsible companies and organizations will never take these types of actions via e-mail.

There are different types of phishing. Common ones include spear phishing and whaling. "Spear phishing" is an attack directed at specific individuals, roles, or organizations. The best defense against spear phishing is to use caution when discarding personal information (i.e., using a cross-cut shredder) that could be used in such an attack. You should also be cognizant of data that may be relatively easily obtained (e.g., your title at work, your favorite places, or where you bank), and think before acting on seemingly random requests via e-mail or phone. For instance, if you receive an e-mail that is curiously vague or written in an uncharacteristic tone or manner, before following the instructions in the e-mail, call or send a separate private e-mail to the sender and confirm that they sent it to you.

"Whaling" is a variation of spear phishing but is directed specifically at executive officers or other high-profile targets within a business, government, or other organization.

Another way to avoid or reduce your exposure to phishing scams is by reading your e-mail as plain text instead of enabling Hypertext Markup Language (HTML). Phishing messages often contain clickable images that look legitimate. If you read the message in plain text, you can see the uniform resource locator (URL) to which any image points. Additionally, when you allow your mail client to read HTML or other non-text-only formatting, attackers can take advantage of your mail client's ability to execute code, which leaves your computer vulnerable to viruses, worms, and Trojans (forms of malware that can cause you an infinite amount of aggravation, time, and expense).

DEALING WITH THE RISK OF IDENTITY THEFT

Many people fear dealing with the Internet or transacting business on it as a result of concerns over identity theft or the theft of personal information that will allow the bad guys to use your credit, access your accounts, or steal your property. We cannot deny that those risks exist. While you do cut down some of your exposure by hiding from the Internet as much as possible, you still do not completely insulate yourself from such risk, and the protection that it gives you does not usually outweigh the inconvenience associated with isolating yourself by not using the Internet.

While we still find plenty of cases of the bad guys sending malicious e-mail attachments, setting up fraudulent websites, and trying to trick you into giving them your personal information, the greatest danger to your assets comes from third parties possessing your information, which they store online, even if you do not.

Unless you have been marooned on a desert island without Internet access and no news media, you have likely heard of some of the numerous major security breaches associated with all levels of government, major companies, and commercial activities.

In September 2017, Equifax (you know, the company that has almost everyone's personal information) revealed that a cyber break-in resulted in the exposure of personal information (including names, Social Security numbers, birth dates, home addresses, and in some cases driver's license numbers—everything a bad guy would need to access your credit). The reports indicated that the breach affected more than 145 million consumers, primarily in the United States, but also in Canada and Great Britain. Subsequent reports indicated that the breach actually affected even more data than Equifax initially disclosed and that it exposed tax identification numbers, e-mail addresses, and additional license information—such as the state of issuance and the issue date.

On April 2, 2018, the *Wall Street Journal* reported that the iconic Hudson's Bay Company's holdings of Lord & Taylor and Saks suffered major data breaches resulting in approximately 5,000,000 valid credit card numbers being available for sale on the Dark Web.

These couple of examples represent only the tip of the iceberg. The bottom line: in today's society, you have exposure to identity theft, whether or not you use the cloud, e-mail, online banking, Facebook, Twitter, Dropbox, or any other piece of the Internet. More importantly, you have no real way to protect yourself from it. The solution: everyone should consider (we think have) insurance against such loss. We use the term literally in this context; we do not just mean taking precautions to try to limit your exposure (although you should, of course, do that), we mean an actual insurance policy.

You can find numerous policies to choose from respecting these risks. We have not evaluated all of them and make no recommendation other than that you look into such coverage and acquire it. We do think you will find the services that provide both insurance against loss and assistance in making proper notifications and taking actions to protect your identity once you learn of a breach that might affect it will serve you better than those that just provide coverage for economic loss. The correction and cleanup issues associated with identity theft can prove time consuming and expensive. Better to let someone who has done it and knows what has to be done handle it than to try to figure it out yourself.

JEFF'S AND ASHLEY'S FAVORITE APPS

OUR FAVORITE APPS

First, we want you to know that when we talk about apps in the context of technology, we refer to software programs or applications, not appetizers. Because so many of us have grown increasingly dependent on our mobile devices (almost all of which run on the iOS or the Android platform these days), no book of technology tips would be complete without touching on a list of recommended apps.

Accordingly, we chose to end our book with a collection of our favorite applications. You can download each application discussed in this chapter in the Google Play Store and/or Apple's iTunes App Store. We will tell you which of the listed applications comes from what store to make it easier for you to choose what you want and to find it. We do not represent that the applications in this chapter are the "best" applications available for each platform. We simply tell you that these apps live on our devices and we use them and like them.

Some of the applications we identify will work on tablets and others on smartphones.

Some will work on both, although often the appearance and functionality will vary among different devices.

Some of the listed applications come free (although free apps often come with the hidden price of forcing you to watch advertisements occasionally). Others will cost you something. Most do not cost very much, but some cost in the $100 range.

In preparing the list, we intentionally excluded applications built into the operating system (such as browsers or Apple's Mail or Calendar program). We may include programs dealing with the same features, if we prefer them over the applications built into the operating system, as nothing requires that you use the applications built into the system if you find others you prefer. Sometimes third parties have a better take on how to do a particular thing than folks at Apple or Google. Often, however, it simply comes down to what you prefer. Functionality of apps, like beauty, rests in the beholder's eye!

We have not listed the apps in any particular order or even tried to group them by subject. We have simply identified some of the applications we use regularly and have given you a short description of why we do and what it does.

If we somehow missed your favorite app, let us know. Perhaps we had an issue with it. Perhaps we simply have not found it yet (there are just shy of a gazillion apps on the two platforms combined and we do not claim to have tested every one of them or even to have seen every one of them). If you tell us about an app we have not encountered, and we include it in our next volume of *Technology Tips for Seniors*, we will happily autograph your copy of the next volume of *Technology Tips for Seniors*.

JEFF'S FAVORITE APPS

1. **Microsoft Word**. The Microsoft Word app allows your mobile device to read and write to Word documents. It works with tablets and smartphones (but better with tablets). It comes for both the iOS and Android platforms. Word has become the de facto standard for word processing in and out of the legal profession. You can get the app free but limited to read only. If you want full functionality, you need a subscription to Microsoft Office 365.

2. **Microsoft PowerPoint**. The Microsoft PowerPoint app allows your mobile device to read and write to PowerPoint files and to use PowerPoint for presentations directly from your mobile device. It works with tablets and smartphones (but better with tablets). It comes for both the iOS and Android platforms. PowerPoint has become the de facto standard for presentations in and out of the legal profession. You can get the app free but limited to read only. If you want full functionality, you need a subscription to Microsoft Office 365.

3. **Dropbox**. The Dropbox app allows your mobile device to connect to your Dropbox account and to download and open documents you have stored in Dropbox from your smartphone or tablet. It comes for both Android and iOS devices. If you have and use a Dropbox account, you should have this app on your mobile devices.

4. **VPN Unlimited**. You can set up your own virtual private network

(VPN) or get access to a commercial VPN. VPN Unlimited is a commercial VPN that enables you to use one of its numerous servers to securely connect to the Internet from an insecure hotspot. Available on a subscription basis, often at substantial discounts, the app is also easy to use. It comes on both the iOS and Android platforms and you can even get it to work with your computers.

5. **Kindle**. The Kindle app allows your mobile device to emulate a Kindle e-reader and access your Kindle library. It works very well and ensures that you have access to your library as long as you have any of your compatible mobile devices with you. It works on both smartphones and tablets and comes on both iOS and Android platforms.

6. **Audible**. The Audible app lets you listen to books instead of reading them. It comes in handy if you want to have someone tell you a story while you drive down the highway or if your eyes are tired. It is

available on Android and iOS for smartphones and tablets.

7. **Fitbit**. This app works with your Fitbit wristband and allows you to sync your information to your smartphone and to your Internet account for access by your other devices. It keeps track of your activities, your sleep, your weight, and other vital health information. It is available on iOS and Android, and is designed for smartphones, but also works on tablets. If you have a Fitbit, you should have the app.

8. **Lose-it**. Interested in tracking your calories? Weight? Protein, fat, or carbohydrate intake? Get this app. Studies have shown that people who record what they eat accurately do better in terms of weight loss. I have not found an app that I think does that job better or easier than Lose-it. The app is available on Android and iOS, and is designed for smartphones, but also works on tablets.

9. **OpenTable**. OpenTable helps you find good restaurants throughout the United States. After you make your

selection, you can use the app to make reservations. OpenTable will recommend restaurants based on price, cuisine, and location. It also provides you with access to the menu for most of the restaurants it lists. The app also presents reviews from restaurant guests to help you make your decision. It is available for Android and iOS. It has led us to some very excellent restaurant choices.

10. **GoogleMaps**. The app was designed by Google for its Android system, but is also available for iOS devices. It is an excellent map and Global Positioning System (GPS)-based guidance system to get you from one place to another using private vehicles, public transportation, bicycles, or your feet. It will show you the route and give you step-by-step audio directions. It works in the United States and abroad. It will also estimate the travel time. The Google Play Store summarizes the features of the app as follows:

> Offline maps to search, get directions and use navigation without an internet connection.

Street View and indoor imagery for restaurants, shops, museums and more.

Indoor maps to quickly find your way inside big places like airports, malls and stadiums.

Comprehensive, accurate maps in 220 countries and territories.

Transit schedules and maps for over 15,000 cities.

Detailed business information on over 100 million places.

11. **Sygic**. Excellent off-line worldwide GPS navigation system with downloadable maps. The app works with Android and iOS. Never leave the country without it.

12. **GoodReader**. The app works with phones and tablets, for iOS only. GoodReader gives you a powerful PDF reader with lots of features to make your life easier. It handles large files easily and mark-up documents. It will also let you sign documents. This is one of the best overall PDF readers we have found.

13. **Adobe Acrobat**. Adobe Acrobat offers a similar feature set to

GoodReader, but is also available for the Android platform. Some features work as well as GoodReader, others better, and others not as well. Also, the app will convert PDF files to editable Word and Excel files. It is worth the trouble of having both.

14. **Adobe Photoshop Fix**. This is a good, basic photo editor and retouching tool that works on Android and iOS, smartphones and tablets. Note this is not a full-fledged photoshop. It simply offers you the ability to fine tune your images.

15. **Lumosity**. Lumosity offers a collection of puzzles and activities designed to help keep your brain active and sharp. Many come in the form of fairly entertaining games. Everyone should have this app; but it does nothing if you do not use it. Regularly use it and it should help keep you sharp. It certainly cannot hurt anything. It works on Android and iOS, smartphones and tablets.

16. **HP 12C**. I am old school. The first pocket (briefcase-sized) calculators hit

the market while I was in law school. Several years later, Hewlett-Packard (HP) introduced its HP 12C financial calculator, which most people in the financial industry quickly recognized as the best thing since sliced bread. Of course, I got one and used it for years. In fact, I still have one. But more recently, I need not carry it around with me, as I can get apps that emulate the HP 12C brilliantly. I have found numerous emulations in the Google Play Store and the Apple iTunes App Store. I have not tried them all, but I have tried several. The one I use has a gold and black logo in the store that simply says "hp" on one line and "12C" below that. It costs $14.99 in the Google Play Store. Others that I have tried worked about as well, but this one provides what I consider the best emulation of my favorite calculator of all time. In the 40 years or so that I have used the 12C or its emulation app, I have never found a real estate or financial calculation that I needed to do that it could not handle.

17. **Skype**. This app is available on
    Android and iOS on phones and tab-
    lets to use for video calls without
    regard to whether the other person
    or people involved are using iOS
    or Android devices. Skype works
    well locally, nationally, and interna-
    tionally if you have decent Internet
    access. We have even seen Skype
    used for long-distance depositions
    (we have mixed reactions to the pro-
    cess and it is not our favorite way to
    take depositions).

18. **FileMaker Go**. FileMaker Go is for
    iOS only. This provides a mobile
    companion to the FileMaker data-
    base software. If you need a database
    program for general use, FileMaker
    has established itself as one of the
    best. If you want the data available
    for mobile access and use, you need
    this app. If you do not have File-
    Maker on your computer and/or do
    not use it, do not bother with this
    app, as it will do you no good.

19. **Flixster**. This app keeps us up to
    date on what movies we can and
    should see. It is location sensitive

and can tell you what theaters you can find near almost anywhere you are in the continental United States. It tells you what movies you can see at that theater and what times the movies play. If you have questions, it provides an intro to the movie and can even show you a trailer. The app will also tell you what movies will come out in the future and when. If you like movies, you want this app on your smartphone. It works on iOS and Android.

20. **Bank of America**. Online banking has grown into a very valuable set of services. Most banks' apps let you pay bills, check balances, make deposits, and transfer funds. Although the interfaces differ, most seem to do pretty much the same thing. It is like having a bank branch in your pocket. The only thing these apps cannot do is disburse cash to you. For that you need a brick-and-mortar branch or an automated teller machine (ATM). This app works only with Bank of America. I do not particularly think its features are better than other banks, but

it is one bank I use, so I use the app a lot. Put whatever bank(s) you use on your mobile devices. This one is available for iOS and Android.

21. **Wells Fargo**. This is Wells Fargo bank's mobile app offering. The description and operation are pretty much the same as Bank of America's app, but it only works for Wells Fargo customers. It is available for iOS and Android, smartphones and tablets.

22. **Atari's Greatest Hits**. The first computer games came out as arcade games from companies like Atari. This app, available on iOS and Android, will give you access to most of the best (and some of the not so great) Atari arcade games of yesteryear. It includes classics like Centipede, Androids, Space Invaders, Breakout, Missile Command, Pong, and Lunar Lander. For a trip back in time, you cannot beat this.

23. **Pinball HD Collection**. Another great pastime from yesteryear, pinball has made a digital return. You can find lots of pinball game variations for both Android and iOS

devices. I am partial to the Pinball HD (for high definition) Collection. It gives you several versions of pinball games and you can get it for iOS or Android. It works on both smartphones and tablets, but plays better on tablets due to their size. Even the new larger screen smartphones do not offer a sufficient display size for what I consider a comfortable use of the pinball apps.

24. **News**. You can find a tremendous number of news apps on both the Android and iOS platforms. Some are quite useful. One of my favorites (comes from Apple and is part of the iOS system—sorry Android users) goes by the name "News" and works as an aggregator of news stories to give you short headlines of top stories and trending news events. You can find other apps that will aggregate news for you on both the Android and iOS platforms (check out Flipboard, for example, on either platform). Flipboard, incidentally is quite good; I just like News better.

News gives you the headlines and will provide more information including the entire article if you want to see it. It will also give you some very entertaining videos. This is a great way to have your news delivered on your iOS device anywhere you have Internet access.

25. **Magzter**. We discuss this app as a tip in the Miscellaneous Technology Tips chapter of this book. I included it here because it is one of my favorites, as I like to read information about how other countries see us.

26. **OmniOutliner**. Available on iOS only, OmniOutliner provides a solid and reliable outlining capability to your iOS devices. It makes it easy to create and modify your outlines. You can find a lot of outlining apps on both platforms, but if you like using outlines and use iOS devices, check this one out.

27. **theScore**. If you like to follow professional and/or collegiate sports, you have likely discovered that you have many choices of apps on the Android

and iOS platforms to help you follow and enjoy current sporting events. I have several on my devices, but this one stands out as one of my favorites due to its versatility. The Play Store description notes that it provides

> collegiate and professional coverage of many sports (including all major sports). It provides you with news, scores, stats, and videos from NBA Basketball, NCAA Basketball, MLB Baseball, NFL Football, NCAA Football, NHL Hockey, English Premier League Soccer, La Liga Soccer, Champions League Soccer, FIFA World Cup, PGA Golf—including The Masters—and every major league and competition.

I enjoy knowing the stats during a game to help me appreciate it better. The app provides detailed statistical information on a current basis in the game (only a few seconds of lag time provided you have a good Internet connection). You can pick your favorite teams and get updates on those teams. You can even get a play-by-play feed on many games. It is available on iOS and Android.

28. **Duolingo**. Duolingo is an entertaining way to kill some time and learn some basic phrases in a language. It offers numerous languages and can come in handy in getting ready to travel overseas. English has not yet become universal (mostly there, but still a way to go). The app has Android and iOS availability.

29. **Voice Translator**. This is great for travel. It lets you (or someone with whom you are trying to communicate) speak into the phone in one language and it translates to another. It uses voice and text. This one costs $7.99/week if you do not cancel it, so you will want to turn it on and off when you travel to ensure that you only pay for it while you travel. I have this on iOS. I could not find the same app on the Android platform. There is a program called Voice Translator 2017 on the Android platform. It does not have as many languages (only 27) but does the same

thing with spoken language and comes free.

30. **TripIt**. TripIt is the best travel app I have found for keeping track of your plans. You can send it airline reservations, hotel reservations, and other information, and it will organize it all for you and create a calendar for your travel. You can share that calendar with others who need to have the information. They have a free version and a pro version (subscription). The pro version gives you information on flight situations and also lets you know if there is a fare change on one of your flights.

31. **Southwest**. Major airlines and most regional carriers have their own apps now. These apps help you make reservations, check in for your flight, verify flight status, schedule and check on your frequent flier accounts with that airline, check weather alerts, and modify your flight information. They also provide you with the ability to check in using your phone for a boarding pass. Southwest's app is not necessarily

better than others, but it is an airline I fly regularly, so it lives on my
devices and I use it often. It is available on Android and iOS.

32. **United**. See the comments about
the Southwest app above. United
is another carrier I use frequently,
so I have its app on my phone. If
you fly United and plan to use their
Wi-Fi to stream entertainment, you
must have the current version of the
United app. It is also available on
iOS and Android.

33. **GateGuru**. This is a useful travel app
that provides maps and guides for
more than 200 airports throughout
the United States, Canada, Europe,
Asia, and Australia. It shows you how
to get to your gate and what shopping
and food services you will find near
your gate. It also tells you where to
find the place you are looking for at
the airport (assuming the airport has
such a facility), whether it is a nail
salon, a Brookstone, or a Starbucks. It
is available on Android and iOS.

34. **Dragon Anywhere**. Dragon Anywhere helps you create, edit, format,

and share documents using your Android or iOS mobile device from just about anywhere that you have an Internet connection. Dragon Anywhere lets you dictate and edit documents by voice on your iOS or Android mobile device quickly and fairly accurately, helping you stay productive anywhere you go. If you do not want to invest in or carry professional dictation equipment but want to use speech to text on the road, this offers a good solution. If you have Dragon for the Mac or Dragon Naturally Speaking on your computer, it works even better, as you can move the files from one device to another and use them on your mobile device and your computer. Use of the app on a mobile device has not proven as accurate as Dragon for the Mac or Dragon Naturally Speaking using a quality microphone or professional dictation equipment, but for general use, it works pretty well. You can try it free for a week. After that you have to subscribe if you want to use it. The cost is $150/year or $15/month. If your fingers do not work as well on the miniature keyboards as you would like, this offers a decent fix for a reasonable price. Even if you type quickly on the device keyboards, it can speed up production enough to easily pay for it at your standard hourly rates. Remember, if you bill $150/hour or more, it has only to save you one hour of time during a year to break even and anything more than that is profit.

35. **Flipboard**. Flipboard, like Apple's News app, curates news stories from all over the world to help give information important to you respecting those events. They advertise that the app lets you "focus on what matters to you, not the random posts of other people's lives." I consider it fairly comparable to Apple's News app and used it more extensively before Apple's News app was available. As this works on both Android and iOS devices (while Apple's News app

works on iOS only), if you have an Android device, this should be the go-to news aggregator. It costs nothing, so try it and see if you like it. When you first start out, you will need to set up an account (a couple of minutes) and tell the app what interests you have. It will then provide a digital magazine created for you from articles that relate to your chosen subject areas.

36. **The Great Courses**. For those of you unfamiliar with the Great Courses, it is the brand used by the Teaching Company to market its (mostly) college-level programs. You can get excellent programs in multiple areas of interest presented by leading academicians from major colleges and universities for very reasonable prices. You can access their website at https://www.thegreatcourses.com/. You can buy their courses at substantial discounts over their retail pricing, as they always have a sale in progress. Just wait for the rotation to get to

the programs you want. Some programs come in audio only, while others come in video format. You can get the programs (depending on the program) as downloads. Once you buy a program, it goes into your digital library and you can listen to it online using your computer or on a mobile device using the app. They also have a second app (the Great Courses Plus) for their subscription Great Courses Plus program. The difference with the subscription is that you buy no programs (or at least you need not buy any) and simply stream any of their library of programs to your device. If you plan on making yourself a lifelong learner, consider the subscription, as it will save you a lot of money. Both of these apps work on iOS and Android devices and you can access the courses on your computer through your browser.

37. **TranscriptPad**. Designed primarily for litigators, this app works only on the iPad. I have found no good

equivalent on the Android platform. If you practice litigation, this app may be a good enough reason to cause you to get an iPad. The app lets you review and mark up legal transcripts quickly and efficiently. You can highlight, flag, underline, comment on, and issue code the transcript using the app. Currently, it comes as a one-time purchase; however, there are rumors that the three apps from this developer (Transcript-Pad, DocReviewPad, and TrialPad) will convert to a subscription basis in the not too distant future along with the addition of a fourth (as yet not officially named) program to build time lines.

38. **DocReviewPad**. Designed primarily for litigators, this app works only on the iPad. I have found no good equivalent on the Android platform. If you practice litigation, this app may be a good enough reason to cause you to get an iPad. The app lets you import, Bates stamp, review, redact, and zoom in on documents quickly and efficiently. Like TranscriptPad,

DocReviewPad currently comes as a one-time purchase; however, note the comments in the discussion of TranscriptPad respecting that the developer will convert to a subscription model soon.

39. **Inspiration Maps**. Inspiration Maps gives you a simple and easy to use mind-mapping program. For those of you who use mind mapping, you already know what a powerful tool it can provide. For those who do not, try it and see. The Inspiration Maps program comes free, but is limited to five documents to let you try it out. After that, you need to graduate to Inspiration Maps VPP either through an "in-app" purchase or through purchase of the VPP version directly from the app store. The Inspiration Maps VPP app gives you an unrestricted version that you have to buy for $39.95 or through a subscription. The app only comes for iOS, but you can get computer programs from the same company for both the MacOS and Windows. The software was designed for the educational market

but works anywhere you want to use mind mapping as a graphic outline or brainstorming tool.

40. **Evernote**. If you have ever wondered where you should store information that you will want to access later, Evernote has the answer. Evernote gives you an organizer and planner notebook that lets you take notes, scan documents, add sketches to your notes, add images, and more. You can organize your work lists, projects, and programs in Evernote. You can sync to the cloud and transfer the information among your devices. Evernote works on iOS and Android mobile devices and on your computer. You set up one account and connect all your devices to it and they share the information once you sync it.

41. **TextExpander**. TextExpander works on the Mac and Windows operating systems and iOS. There is not an Android version. It gives you the ability to save a lot of time and effort. You set up abbreviations

of a few characters and when you type them the program expands the characters into whatever text you have coded into that abbreviation. It takes a little effort to set up but works easily and well. You can cut and paste a paragraph or several and then assign a couple of characters and move on to the next shortcut. For example, whenever I type "yt," TextExpander types a letter closing consisting of "Yours truly, Jeffrey Allen." Typing "lof" gets me the name of the firm and the address of my office. I have some longer expansions (some a line or two and others several paragraphs), but it will not help to insert them here, as you get the idea. It comes in particularly handy for certain repetitive forms such as contract terms or portions of pleadings. The software used to exist as a stand-alone but recently converted to a subscription basis (it costs less than $40/year). If you have the subscription version and connect the app to the Internet, snippets you include on one device will automatically transfer to your other devices linked to the same account. They have two versions, the single person version and the team version. The team version will allow your staff to link to the same account and share shortcuts.

42. **Scrabble**. I doubt I have to explain the game of Scrabble to anyone reading this book. When younger, I used to carry a travel-sized version of the game when we went on vacation. I have always liked the game and I think it helps keep my mind sharp. You pit your vocabulary skills against those of the computer, which you can set to different levels. If you can win more games than you lose at the highest skill level for the computer, that is a pretty good achievement. Note that you lose your records when you upgrade from one device to another. The Scrabble app does give you the option of playing opponents other than the computer, and even finding them online. I am not

as impressed with that aspect of the app, preferring to use it solely for me versus the computer games.

43. **Words with Friends**. This is my app of choice for playing the equivalent of Scrabble online with others. I think they have done a good job organizing this and providing a variety of structures and opponents. It seems popular and there appears to be an almost endless supply of opponents available. It also has practice opportunities that are you versus the computer style games. Note this does not offer traditional Scrabble. The board and the rules, while similar, diverge substantially from traditional Scrabble.

44. **Boggle**. Another great game from the Words with Friends folks. This is a variation of the board game that lets you spell out as many words as you can from a group of letters. You can play in practice mode against the computer or against people online. Either way offers a good challenge to help keep your mind sharp.

ASHLEY'S FAVORITE APPS

1. **Viber**. Viber is a communication app that allows users to exchange instant messages and place calls over Wi-Fi. It is a useful tool when traveling abroad, allowing you to stay in touch with other Viber users back home whenever you are connected.

2. **Workfrom**. This app is very useful for business travelers, even when traveling in your own city. The app crowdsources locations that are ideal for getting work done on the road. Users identify places with free Wi-Fi, access to power outlets, and table surface space where you can set up and work comfortably for a long period of time. You can rate noise and crowd level, and add information like the wireless Internet name and password. You can also add location information and helpful details like whether coffee, food, or alcoholic beverages are available and at what hours, so fellow users can

find the ideal place to work while they are on the road.

3. **Yummly**. If you are looking for new recipes or ways to stay on your diet, Yummly is a useful tool for your kitchen. The app offers users access to share recipes and ways to search by ingredients or diet restrictions.

4. **Pinterest**. This app and website has revolutionized the way we DIY (do-it-yourself), whether it is fashion, interior design, arts and crafts, recipes, or more, you can find links, articles, and comments to thousands of ideas. Pinterest allows you to "pin" these ideas to custom boards so you can organize your project ideas in a single space, sort of like an inspiration board.

5. **PayPal**. This app and website facilitates economic exchanges between users. For a fee, businesses can collect payment for goods or services. It also allows you to send money from a bank without a fee to friends and family. This is a fast and cost-efficient alternative to Western Union.

6. **Venmo**. Venmo is a mobile payment service, similar to PayPal. Oddly enough, it is now owned by PayPal. It is like a social payment transfer site: users can see when their friends transfer money to each other. It is popular with the millennial and later generations.

7. **LogMeOnce**. This app is a handy password manager with two-factor authentication that is available for iOS and Android smartphones. It even employs password-less log-ins, allowing you to snap a selfie and use photo-login, or set up a fingerprint scan.

8. **Pocket Wine Journal**. This app is like a diary for wine lovers. If you find a wine you like and want to remember it for later, you can snap a picture of it and enter in details about the varietal, along with notes on what you like about the wine (depending on how much time you have in the moment). It is a great way to preserve the memory before too many glasses of said wine take effect.

9. **ShopWell**. This app can help you choose better foods while you are at the grocery store. You can scan the bar code on more than 350,000 products and find out their health ratings. No more relying on product packaging.

10. **Vipon**. Vipon is an app and web service for Amazon shoppers looking for even greater discounts. The site allows sellers to offer coupon codes so users can buy and try their product at a steep discount. At one time, this was done in exchange for a positive review, but that requirement has since been lifted, making it more like a coupon-clipping site for Amazon shoppers.

11. **Vivino**. With Vivino, you can take a photo of any wine label and learn about the wine's rating, reviews, and average price instantly. No more guessing at the grocery store.

12. **Waze**. Waze is a crowdsourced GPS tool. It is like social media navigation. Wazers (users of Waze) create an account, choose their emoji (the app

provides a variety to suit your mood), and off they go, providing data via satellite on traffic conditions in their area. Users can submit details about traffic by reporting on conditions, such as heavy traffic, accidents, and road closures, that the app then uses to adjust the route, minimizing your time spent in traffic.

13. **WTForecast**. This app presents a humorous report on your local weather. It makes checking the weather entertaining, with quips on how miserably cold or spring-like it might be outside. You can add different areas to get reports of current conditions in other cities.

14. **QR Scanner**. This free app allows users to scan Quick Response (or QR) codes and to connect to the website to which a code was intended to direct them. It is a useful tool depending on how many QR codes you encounter.

15. **LoungeBuddy**. This app compiles information on airport lounges in your area, including who may access them, their hours of operation, the

cost for one-day entry, and what amenities the lounge provides. It is particularly useful if you find yourself stuck in an airport for an extended length of time.

16. **Wordly**. Wordly is a fun word game that runs in three-minute intervals, a good way to pass the time if you find yourself on hold over the phone. The game presents a series of letters and asks you to connect the letters to those adjacent to it, forming as many words as possible in the time allotted.

17. **The Battle of Polytopia**. This turn-based civilization-building game is a fun way to pass the time, especially if you suffer from airplane anxiety (like this author) and need a distraction during takeoff and landing. You can play in perfection mode, which limits you to 30 turns to conquer as much as you can. Domination mode runs until you are the total conqueror, or are conquered. Either way, a full game takes about 40 minutes, just enough time to get up in the air.

18. **Pandora**. Pandora is a streaming music app that allows users to play music similar to particular artists or songs that they enjoy. The app employs an algorithm to predict what you would like to listen to based on the artist or song you requested, and hones that prediction by offering you a thumbs up or down button. Clicking the thumbs down on a song will stop it playing immediately and remove it from your library (although it will not stop variations of the same song, like the acoustic version or a remake, from popping up in your playlist again).

19. **Nike + Run Club**. This app is powered by Nike. It will track and log your runs, along with data on how each run went. It works with the Apple Watch. One of the best features of this app (even if you do not use the Apple Watch for data collection) is the collection of guided runs. This collection offers audio guidance during a run that can be generally motivational, or compelling you to

speed up or slow down in set intervals for a better workout. It is a great training tool for runners.

20. **JustWatch**. If you have ever wanted to watch a movie or television show, but were not sure where you could watch it, then JustWatch will be useful for you. This app will search for the streaming services that offer the show you are interested in, and display the cost. This saves you from having to go to each site and do a search for the show there.

21. **GoodRx** Prescription drugs can get expensive. GoodRx can help. With this app you can search all the pharmacies in the area to find out how much each is charging for a drug without insurance. It will also notify you if any coupons are available for the drug.

22. **FreePrints**. This app is a quick and easy way to turn the digital images taken on your phone or tablet into physical, printed photos. You can review, edit, and order prints stored on your device within the app, and

have them mailed directly to your house. The app gives you a certain number of free 4 inch × 6 inch prints every month, but you can also order different sizes and finishes for a marginal cost. If you stick with the free print size and number, then all you will pay is shipping. At the start of the next month, you will get a number of free prints again.

23. **Speedtest**. Speedtest will test the Internet performance of the network to which you are connected. If you want to see how fast your Internet really is, just download the app from the iOS, Google Play, Amazon, or Windows store, open it, and the app will automatically check the speed of whatever network you are connected with, including Wi-Fi and cellular networks.

24. **Goodreads**. Goodreads is a "social cataloging" website that allows users to search its database of books, annotations, and reviews. Users can create their own profile, connect with friends through social media, add

books that they have read or want to read, and receive recommendations to help them discover new authors.

25. **AppZapp**. This app lets you set alerts and search for apps that are now free or have gone on sale. You can designate the type of app you are looking for (games, utility, and so on) and whether you want to be alerted when they go on sale or only if they become free. AppZapp will monitor the App Store and compile a list daily.

26. **CamCard**. CamCard helps you manage business cards. You can scan a card into your contacts using the camera on your smartphone and capture the information the moment you receive it, improving the odds of making a meaningful follow-up connection.

27. **FamCal**. This app is a shared family planner that helps you keep track of everyone's schedule, as well as shared to-do lists and notes.

28. **Prime Photos**. This app provides cloud storage for photos to Amazon

Prime users. You can print the photos at a cost and have them delivered to you with free Prime shipping, which actually works out to about the same cost per print as FreePrints. The cloud storage feature is a handy way to preserve your photographic memories without filling up your device's memory and risking losing them in a catastrophic loss.

29. **Trello**. Trello is an app to manage tasks and keep groups organized. The app can also be accessed over the web. You can set up boards to manage projects or lists, add additional users to each board, and assign tasks to those users, or color code their priority. It can be handy for office teams and families alike.

30. **Zillow**. Zillow is a real-estate and home-value aggregator. It allows users to view real estate data in designated areas or you can have it set to pull up data that is around you. It is a fun way to get familiar with an area you are exploring, or to plan your next move.

31. **Petfinder**. This app can help you find your new furry best friend. It is a search site for adoptable pets with a ton of useful features for finding the perfect addition to your family.

32. **Airbnb**. This is a home-sharing website and app that allows users to offer up rooms or whole homes as a place to stay for travelers. Homes are reviewed by travelers who have visited the place. You can search for a place to stay with a number of filters to make finding your home-away-from-home simple and low-cost.

33. **HomeAway**. This is another home-sharing app, which is a competitor to Airbnb (though you will sometimes find the same homes listed on both). It was formerly known as VRBO (which stood for Vacation Rentals by Owner).

34. **Yelp**. Yelp is an app and website that makes finding places easy and fun. You can read reviews and see pictures and find details on local businesses. It is a handy tool for finding a place to eat when you are in a new

place, as well as for finding area attractions.

35. **Credit Karma**. This app and web service allows users to easily monitor their credit reports for free. You can check your credit score, see any changes and what might be causing the change, and identify ways to improve your score. You can also research credit cards before you apply as well as loan services in your area.

36. **Doodle**. Doodle is an app and web service that makes scheduling easier by generating polls so users can get feedback on what times are available, providing an easy view of what time and day would work best. You do not have to be a registered user to access the poll and respond, making it accessible to anyone with Internet access and e-mail.

37. **Groupon**. Groupon is an app and web service that allows users to shop for discounted goods and experiences. You can search for

experiences close to you, as well as services such as hair salons and spa services, or you can look at destinations you might be visiting soon. You can find discounts to concerts, restaurants, theme parks, and many other attractions.

38. **Poshmark**. This app is similar to eBay, and is a great place to shop gently used laptop bags and travel gear. It focuses primarily on clothes and shoes for women, men, and children.

39. **OverDrive**. This app connects with your local library and allows you to download books in e-book or audiobook format for a set lending period. It is a great way to kill time on a long drive (audiobook) or to catch up on the latest chart-toppers.

40. **BeFunky**. BeFunky is a great way to make photo collages with the images on your phone. You can send the collages to friends and family either via text or e-mail, or upload them to your social media.

41. **Expensify**. Expensify is an app and web-based service that makes managing receipts and expenses easy. Anytime you get a receipt, simply open the app, take a picture with your smartphone, and the app will automatically fill.